This book should be a staple to every administ
for any bookshelf of the novice or seasoned a
home on trust and how trust is essential for
you really want to do anything with an evalt
all angles of why trust and evaluations go ha

D0891343

Jason Eitner, Superintendent
The Lower Alloways Creek School District
Canton Salem, NJ

As administrators, we all deal with evaluations every day. This book
allows you to begin knowing your teachers, but especially knowing
yourself as an evaluator. In order for student growth to make a positive
impact, you, as the instructional leader, need to make a positive impact
with your teachers; this starts with trust and building a better teacher
via evaluations. This book will lead you in that direction!

Elizabeth Alvarez, Principal
John C. Dore Elementary School
Chicago, IL

As school districts across our country are developing and implementing
new teacher evaluation systems, I found Building Trust in Teacher
Evaluations *to be a timely, wonderful, and much-needed resource.*

Dr. Shelly Arneson's use of personal anecdotes as a teacher, counselor,
principal, and consultant, and even as a pet lover, are often shared with
humor and so easy to relate to for anyone who is or has ever been
involved in the school setting. I found myself endlessly nodding in
agreement throughout the chapters. Information based on research is
shared in language free of a lot of educational jargon that contributes
to the reader-friendliness of this book.

If I were still an active assistant superintendent, I would purchase a
copy for each administrator in my district and make arrangements for
us to do a mandatory book study together. During our book study, we
would discuss the value of the principals following suit with their own
building-level book studies of Building Trust in Teacher Evaluations.

To ensure readers know what to do in order to implement trust-
building and communication strategies straightaway, Dr. Arneson's
book provides easy-to-use, common-sense approaches and examples

practical to the educational field, especially with our current national prominence on developing and implementing new teacher evaluation systems.

Linda D. Goodwin, Consultant
The Danielson Group
Crosset, AR

School personnel—administrators, teachers, and support staff—need to be reminded about the immensely important role that trust and effective communication play in school culture and climate, and this book addresses that point quite well.

Victoria Childs, Assistant Professor
Department of Teacher Education,
University of Illinois Springfield
Springfield, IL

Dr. Arneson's research-based Building Trust in Teacher Evaluations *is an effective and practical guide for those interested in building trust and creating a more authentic and fertile evaluation environment. Every school leader interested in improved communication and improved teacher performance should read and heed!*

Lee Hale, Principal
Meigs Middle School
Shalimar, FL

As a teacher leader with over 30 years of experience, I found Chapter 5 of Dr. Arneson's book ("Teach the Process") to be the best advice any district could follow to build solid trust among all stakeholders in communicating the truth about the evaluation process. If teachers are well-informed participants, they will be actively involved and everyone will learn from one another to advance practices of teaching.

Teresa A. Lien, Instructional Facilitator
Baraboo School District, Wisconsin

As school leaders stand at the threshold of a world of mandated changes, Dr. Arneson offers real life scenarios and applicable strategies for strengthening trust and communication between school administration and teachers.

Dr. Arneson's proactive approach to trust and communication should be explored by all school leaders who are not only focusing on the everyday challenging tasks of a school administrator, but for those administrators who are ready to reflect and strengthen their own practices.

Dr. Arneson's unparalleled and profound insight on trust and communication is a testament for all school leaders to explore.

Michelle Vaughn, Assistant Professor
Mercer University, Henry Regional Academic Center
McDonough, Georgia

To Dave, my husband, best friend and soul mate, for whom my trust knows no bounds.

BUILDING TRUST

in Teacher Evaluations

It's not what you say;

it's how you say it

SHELLY M. ARNESON

Foreword by Charlotte Danielson

CORWIN
A SAGE Company

FOR INFORMATION:

Corwin

A SAGE Company

2455 Teller Road

Thousand Oaks, California 91320

(800) 233-9936

www.corwin.com

SAGE Publications Ltd.

1 Oliver's Yard

55 City Road

London EC1Y 1SP

United Kingdom

SAGE Publications India Pvt. Ltd.

B 1/I 1 Mohan Cooperative Industrial Area

Mathura Road, New Delhi 110 044

India

SAGE Publications Asia-Pacific Pte. Ltd.

3 Church Street

#10-04 Samsung Hub

Singapore 049483

Executive Editor: Arnis Burvikovs

Senior Associate Editor: Desirée A. Bartlett

Associate Editor: Ariel Price

Project Editor: Veronica Stapleton Hooper

Copy Editor: Lana Todorovic-Arndt

Typesetter: C&M Digitals (P) Ltd.

Proofreader: Jennifer Grubba

Indexer: Jeanne R. Busemeyer

Cover Designer: Gail Buschman

Marketing Manager: Lisa Lysne

Copyright © 2015 by Corwin

Printed in the United States of America.

Library of Congress Cataloging-in-Publication Data

Arneson, Shelly.

Building trust in teacher evaluations : it's not what you say; it's how you say it / Shelly M. Arneson; foreword by Charlotte Danielson.

pages cm

Includes bibliographical references and index.

ISBN 978-1-4833-1977-3 (alk. paper)

1. Teachers—Rating of—United States. 2. Communication in education—United States. 3. Trust—United States. I. Title.

LB2838.A763 2014

371.14′00973—dc23   2014013685

This book is printed on acid-free paper.

14 15 16 17 18 10 9 8 7 6 5 4 3 2 1

Contents

Chapter 1: Introduction   1

With the author's research on trust as a foundation, the importance of a relationship built on trust between teachers and school leaders will be explored. Definitions and basic research surrounding trust are also examined, as well as their impact on schools.

Chapter 2: Evaluations Done "With"
**   Teachers, Not "to" Teachers**   15

How do we move from traditional observation and evaluation models in which teachers are observed and then "given" a rating? This chapter explores the possibilities of how teacher evaluations done with teachers can move teacher growth by expanding their repertoire of strategies, collaborating with administrators and peers, and learning more about their own practice. Examples are also given about how school leaders can model the learning process.

Chapter 3: Building Teacher Trust and
**   Communication in the Evaluation Process**   25

The author's own research on trust revealed communication to be the number one factor in building trust. The research linking communication and trust is also shared, along with possible solutions to communication barriers.

Chapter 4: Builder 1—Build Relationships, Not an Empire   33

If relationships are to be built on trust, key pieces must be in place for teachers to be able to collaborate with administrators. Factors such as time, openness, and willingness are keys to relationship building and will be discussed in depth.

Chapter 5: Builder 2—Teach the Process   39

Although districts across the country often say they feel as though they are building the new evaluation airplane while it's in the air, this chapter suggests concrete, proactive strategies to get quality training disseminated in the timeliest fashion possible, including how to address dissention and controversy.

Chapter 6: Builder 3—Communicate Objectively   49

Objectivity is one of the keys to success if we are going to build teacher evaluation systems based on honesty and trust. Teachers simply must know that administrators are making decisions based on evidence and facts, versus using opinions, biases, and judgments. Suggestions are shared about how to keep observations and evaluations as objective as possible.

Chapter 7: Builder 4—It's Not What You Say;
It's How You Say It   57

"It's not what you say; it's how you say it" might actually be a subtitle for this book on how to better establish trusting relationships between teachers and school leaders. Strategies to increase the effectiveness of our own communication are shared.

Chapter 8: Builder 5—Follow-Up With
Honesty and Support   69

Post-observation or follow-up conversations may not be required in all districts across the country, but the power of a reflection conversation cannot be denied. Tips for holding effective follow-up conversations are shared, such as being honest, listening to the other person, and sharing strategies for future growth.

Chapter 9: Factors Influencing Trust and Communication 87

Other factors that emerged from the research on trust that influence a trusting relationship and communication include: shared leadership, shared decision making, building capacity in schools, and the school leader's character and competence.

Chapter 10: The Legacy We Leave Behind 101

We have an opportunity to leave behind a legacy of trust and support with every word and action we exhibit with teachers in our schools. Final thoughts about the process by which we maximize the legacy of trust and good communication are shared in this chapter.

Foreword

As every educator recognizes, teaching is enormously complex; teachers make (literally, people have counted this) hundreds of decisions every day. Teaching is demanding, not only physically and emotionally, but cognitively as well. Teaching, in other words, is a *thinking* person's job. And if we accept, and I think we must, that teaching is (among other things) cognitive work, then those who support teachers, in any capacity (mentor, coach, supervisor), must support the *cognition.*

In the framework for teaching, (the FfT), I have broken down this complex work into four main domains of teaching: planning and preparation, the classroom environment, instruction, and professional responsibilities. This framework has helped educators in virtually every state in the United States, and many other countries, acquire a common language and shared understanding about good teaching. This has permitted self-assessment, refection on practice, and professional conversation, all essential contributors to teacher learning.

The most powerful use of the FfT, and the one that should accompany any other use, is for teacher self-assessment and reflection. Even when it is used as the foundation of an evaluation system, it's imperative that structures be in place to promote professional growth. This is because, no matter how successful a lesson is, it could always be at least a little better, and so an approach that permits the analysis of a lesson, around a clear definition of good teaching, is so helpful for promoting learning.

But in order for the FfT (or any other tool) to contribute to professional learning, there must be a culture in the school in which it is safe for teachers to take risks, to try new approaches, and to be critical of their own practice. This culture suggests a need for an environment of trust: Teachers must not fear that their own honest self-appraisal will be used against them. Such an environment is a matter of culture and is a critical ingredient of school leadership.

Learning how to build trust and communication among teachers and school leaders is a necessary ingredient for creating and sustaining a culture that supports teacher growth. The study of trust (and how this trust impacts teacher growth) is what makes Shelly's book so important for teachers, teacher leaders, and administrators alike.

Charlotte Danielson

Preface

66**T**hey won't care what you know until they know that you
care." This profound statement holds true for the teacher's
relationship with the students in the classroom, the faculty member's
relationships with families, and the relationship between educators
and school leaders.

I'd like to begin the book by addressing some questions about
the book and the topic of trust itself.

WHY WRITE A BOOK ON TRUST,
AND WHY WRITE IT NOW?

Trust is vital to every personal and professional relationship we
have, but never was the time so ripe to explore trust in depth than
when states, school districts, and schools were tasked to develop a
new (or embrace an already-developed) evaluation tool. This new
evaluation tool had the added responsibility of being tied to teacher
pay, based on observations and the subsequent evaluation. "How do
we know it will be fair?" was the cry heard around the nation.
Administrators who had previously, in many cases, been managers
of schools were now being asked to talk with teachers about their
teaching more in depth than had previously been required.

While the level of knowledge of the school leader was touted
as very important, perhaps more important became the issue of the
administrator's character. Soon, the issue of trust was emerging as a
critical factor in successful evaluation systems.

As I studied the issue of trust in my educational doctoral program, I was concurrently examining my own past experiences with
administrators and comparing those to the relationships I wanted
(and in most cases, had) with the teachers in the school in which

I was currently the principal. Common themes emerged from my research and from my own practice in implementing the new teacher evaluation system in my own school, and the perfect storm was born.

WHO SHOULD READ THIS?

While teachers will likely find this book incredibly insightful as to what other educators are saying about trust, the primary audiences are school leaders, district leaders, instructional coaches, superintendents, and professors in the area of educational leadership. More and more often, superintendents are sharing the profound need for their principals and assistant principals to have more education in this area. Therefore, universities and colleges across the country would benefit greatly by adding a course designed to improve trust and communication between school leaders and teachers.

WHAT DOES THIS BOOK OFFER?

While talking about trust is interesting on any level of life experience, this text is chock full of strategies based on actual research that will enhance the trust and communication between teachers and school leaders. Tools as simple as word choice and seating arrangement are shared, along with a multitude of others.

The research on trust is substantial and often cited throughout. However, the tone of this book is intended to be conversational. As a colleague mentioned, "In reading pieces of your book, I felt as though we were talking over a cup of coffee." The organization of the book includes an introduction, general information on trust, then a really deep dive into five of the high-impact builders of trust.

By the time you finish reading this book, my fervent hope is that you will have added some possible tools to your toolkit in helping teachers see teacher evaluations as a process that is done with them, collaboratively and in a culture that supports the growth process. You will also find the following:

- Reflection questions to which you can return again and again to evaluate the progress you're making on building trust and communication with your staff
- Strategies for fostering a calm atmosphere in your school
- A process for building a climate of competence among your staff

Acknowledgments

I would love to thank all my cohort members with whom I completed my doctoral program at the University of West Florida and my dissertation chair, Dr. Sherri Zimmerman. I also want to thank Charlotte Danielson and my fellow Danielson consultants, as you have given me the opportunity to do what I love to do in the area of teacher effectiveness. I have learned so much from all of you!

A huge thanks also goes to all the great folks at Corwin Press—Arnis Burvikovs, Ariel Price, Desirée Bartlett, Lana Arndt, and Veronica Hooper—who trusted me with this project and checked my work in a timely yet thorough fashion.

PUBLISHER'S ACKNOWLEDGMENTS

Corwin gratefully acknowledges the contributions of the following reviewers:

Elizabeth Alvarez, Principal
John C. Dore Elementary School
Chicago, IL

Victoria Childs, Assistant Professor
Department of Teacher Education,
University of Illinois Springfield
Springfield, IL

Jay Eitner, Superintendent
The Lower Alloways Creek School District
Canton Salem, NJ

Sharon Lawrence, Assistant Superintendent for Curriculum & Instruction
Averill Park Central School District
Averill Park, NY

Charles L. Lowery, School Principal
Wheat Elementary
Woodville, TX

About the Author

 **Shelly M. Arneson** started as a teacher of students with special needs, became a guidance counselor, and was a principal for 7 years in Florida. Shelly is the author of two other books, *Communicate and Motivate* (2011) and *Letting Go of K.C.* (2011). She graduated with her doctorate in curriculum and instruction from the University of West Florida in August of 2012. Her dissertation was titled *Character and Competence: A Mixed Methods Study on Teacher Trust in a Mid-Sized School District in Northwest Florida.* Shelly and her husband, Dave, have three yellow Labs and currently live in Tucson, Arizona. Shelly is a trainer/consultant with the Danielson Group, and she also works with school districts and organizations to provide workshops and keynote presentations on trust, communication, motivation, and other related topics in education. Shelly enjoys traveling and reading, in addition to writing and learning.

CHAPTER ONE

Introduction

You see, you closed your eyes. That was the difference. Sometimes you cannot believe what you see, you have to believe what you feel. And if you are ever going to have other people trust you, you must feel that you can trust them, too—even when you're in the dark. Even when you're falling.

—Mitch Albom, *Tuesdays with Morrie: An Old Man, a Young Man, and Life's Greatest Lesson*

"Our principal plays favorites, so I am not sure if his evaluation of my teaching is based on actual data or on his impression of me." "How can our principal evaluate our teaching when she only comes in our room one time a year, and the rest of her time is spent in her office with her door shut?" "My principal rated me lower on professionalism because of a parent complaint. But what about my side of the story?" These statements are taken from actual teachers who participated in a survey on trust in their principal (Arneson, 2011a).

The relationship between school principals and teachers is a crucial one for school success. While principals have traditionally been expected to be the school's managers, the principal's role is evolving into a role more accurately described as instructional leader and formal evaluator of teacher practices. For the teacher evaluation process to be effective, teachers must trust the principal's capability and integrity. Likewise, principals need to be able to trust that teachers will hear what they have to say when given honest feedback. Some will say, "Oh, but as long as the principal is trained in using the evaluation model objectively and free from bias, there should be no need to examine trust." The principal's ability and competence in using the evaluation is one factor. The amount of integrity a principal has and uses when observing and evaluating teachers is another factor, and I argue that, in many cases, it is the most important factor. It is also a factor that is difficult to measure. How do you measure how much someone is trusted? How do you really know how much trust is felt in schools? This book will examine those and many more questions.

The new look at the role of principal is a change in the public education system. Covey (1989) defined seven habits that highly effective people use to facilitate change and improve leadership in an organization. One cannot stress enough the importance of forming relationships, building trust, and creating an emotional bank account between people. After studying and using the work of Covey for years in my own administrative experience as a principal, I wanted to study the formation of trust between principal and teacher. I defined and explored trust within the context of competence and character using Covey and Merrill's (2006) trust model. In addition, I also addressed the question of whether there is a relationship between length of time the teacher and principal work together and the perceived level of trust that teachers feel toward the principal. Finally, and in many ways most practical, I asked teachers to identify principal behaviors that would lead to greater trust.

Educational research has the propensity to revolve around the strategies of teaching, methodology of concepts, and management of classrooms in K–12 settings. However, since the principal of a school is the educational leader and, therefore, expected to model effective instructional strategies as well as good communication with parents and positive student interactions, principals and teachers must form a relationship built on trust in order for schools to be truly successful. Trust is an understudied issue. If trust is not present in principal/teacher relationships, it is to the detriment of the schools in which they work. In the United States, a Harris poll in 2005 indicated that only 22% of participants trust the media, 8% trust political parties, 27% trust the United States government, and 12% trust big companies. Only 36% of employees believe their leaders act with integrity (Covey & Merrill, 2006). With these statistics, administrators and school policy makers cannot afford to neglect the aspect of trust. By measuring teacher perceptions of trustworthiness in principals, researchers (Clark & Payne, 2006) can highlight and address leadership strengths and weaknesses, thereby improving school success.

The relationship between school principals and teachers is critical because principals are no longer simply managers of the school building but are performing teacher evaluations that, in many instances, impact teacher pay. For the process to be effective, the principal must be competent and filled with integrity. Some will say, "Oh, but as long as the principal is trained in using the evaluation model objectively and free from bias, there should be no need to examine trust." I beg to differ. In almost every district I visit, the question is raised: Can all the training in the world help a principal truly remain objective?

In schools across the country, the shift of principal roles is from principal as manager to principal as instructional leader. For school communities to make good use of this new type of authority, the quality of relationships will play a major role (Bryk & Schneider, 2002). In light of new teacher evaluation systems basing a percentage of teacher pay on student performance, the trust in school administrators is more critical than before. Districts are using Charlotte Danielson's model of effective teaching, Marzano's (2003) teacher evaluation model, a hybrid of the two, or some other approved system. The district in which I did my research used the evaluation system based on Danielson's (2007) model of enhancing professional teaching practices, defined by four critical domains of the teaching practice, including planning, classroom environment, instructional practices, and professional responsibilities. The evaluation system in many states across the country requires administrators to observe every teacher in the building at least once a year, a significant paradigm shift from the days of tenured teachers in Florida only needing to be observed every 5 years when their teaching certificates were due for renewal (Roberts, 2011). This shift in practice, alone, is enough to raise the hackles of some seasoned teachers who cry out, "Why should we have to be observed every year? Why has it been good enough until now but not good enough any more?" This book does not attempt to address the why's of accountability but rather begins with the point at which we find ourselves: We are here, we are using a new system of evaluation. Now, how are we going to make it more effective, objective, and reliable?

BACKGROUND OF THE PROBLEM

At the beginning of workshops I teach on communication and trust, I often put a speech bubble up on the board with the words, "We have a new evaluation system." I ask participants to think about how they feel about the words in this sentence. I then ask folks to turn and say the sentence to a neighbor. "Say it how you feel it," I ask. I listen in, intent to find some varying example, which I always do. I then play Man on the Street, during which time I ask for volunteers to share how they said the sentence. Inevitably, I can find folks who say the sentence with sarcasm dripping from their smiling voices and others who say it with resignation in their voices and, finally, that group of people who may have perhaps already had too much caffeine that morning who say it with joy and opportunity in their voices.

With the increasing accountability expected from teachers, it is important for principals to help teachers feel more supported to keep quality teachers in the classroom (Rowland, 2008). Danielson (2007) suggests that the observation and evaluation process, typically performed by the principal informing the teacher of strengths and weaknesses of the lesson, should be more collaborative and that this collaboration is going to require trust. As one teacher shared with me, "I am used to the principal pushing the observation form to my side of the desk and asking me if I have any questions. Questions? I thought you would have questions for me about how I make decisions about my teaching." Zimmerman (2003) notes the importance of trust in any principal/teacher evaluative process, so now is the time for administrators to refine their relationship-building skills. Daily interactions in schools need not be dominated by interpersonal conflict, cynicism, and mistrust (Feltman, 2009). Trust impacts schools every day of every year in every relationship and every communication encounter. In every school district in which I consult, teachers and principals express without abandon the concerns they have about miscommunication, tension, mistrust, and more.

Covey (1989), through his seven habits of highly effective people, has aided many business leaders in transforming themselves to encourage growth in the members of their organizations. Schools are not unique in that regard. Major corporations and small businesses around the country have their share of office politics, leaders playing favorite, and misunderstandings that turn to all-out conflict. I've written this book specifically for school leaders, however, because I feel that we are in the business of growing and developing the next generation of adults. My husband and I often play the game of asking, "Would you want this person taking care of us in the nursing home someday?" But it isn't really a game, is it? Growing and developing caring and respectful and thoughtful adults is serious business. And our students watch the staff in the school each and every day. They watch us to see how we are going to handle conflict and other problems. If our students are going to take their lead from us, hadn't we better get it right?

The relationship between principal and teacher is delicate in nature as the principal typically serves as the primary evaluator for the teacher's performance. The relationship, by its very nature, is unbalanced in power. For the teacher to hear what the principal has to say regarding performance, progress, goal setting, and growth, there must be a relationship that allows for effective communication to take place. In workshops across the country, I ask principals, "Do you want to be right or do you want to be heard?" (Arneson, 2011a). The idea behind this is there are two people in the room, both wanting to be heard and both having needs that must be met. Focusing on being heard versus only being right assumes that we are willing to hear the other person as well, not just stamp our foot in our "rightness." In order to do this, we have to possess the willingness to believe that someone else might have a thought that is equally as important to hear as our own. Teachers must believe the principal is fair and equitable in his or her evaluation of teachers' capabilities. Trust is a major factor in relationship building, just as mistrust is a critical factor in the breakdown of relationships.

Contrary to myths about trust being slow to form, nothing seems to be as fast as the speed of trust. I found in talking to teachers around the country that they are quite willing to trust their administrators from the outset. The problem comes in when trust has been violated or is perceived to be violated. The speed of mistrust appears to be rapid, as well. The good news is trust can be created where it is not currently present, but it can also be destroyed where it currently exists. Vodicka (2006) identifies the four elements of trust as (a) compassion, (b) consistency, (c) communication, and (d) competency. Compassion is the caring for other individuals that is central to a trusting relationship. Vodicka says consistency was prevalent in most of the definitions of trust but feels consistency itself was not enough to generate trust. Vodicka found communication to be important as well since leaders whom teachers identified as being open found it was a strategy that bred trust. Competence implies reputation and affiliation, but producing positive results is likely the best determinant of competence.

E-Cubed: Effective Evaluation Example

How do you characterize trust? On which factors
do you feel trust is mainly based?

Feltman (2009) describes trust as taking a risk in exposing oneself and being vulnerable to another person. The four distinct aspects of trust are care, competence, reliability, and sincerity. Feltman describes care as a willingness to show concern for another. Feltman defines competence as the ability level demonstrated to others. Reliability connotes the trustworthiness of a person to do what he or she said he or she would do. Sincerity is also known as authenticity (Feltman, 2009).

Covey (1989) believes individuals form emotional bank accounts with every encounter they have with another person who makes either a deposit or a withdrawal with each meeting. If a principal and teacher have a good relationship, the principal is able to share criticism with the teacher (a withdrawal) and still have enough money in the bank to weather the withdrawal. If the relationship is uncertain or one in which the teacher does not feel comfortable sharing his or her weaknesses or vulnerabilities, there is no savings available from which to withdraw. Trust is easy to lose and hard to regain (Reina & Reina, 2006). Indeed, trust has the potential to create success, but its power is so often underestimated. I often ask workshop participants to imagine a coworker with whom they possess a high level of trust.

I then ask them to characterize what working on a project with that person looks like. They often will say things like "it's easy," "it's fun," "time flies when we work together," and "I don't have to second guess what I am going to say." Working with people whom we trust makes work simpler and more enjoyable.

How, then, do principals and teachers build up this trust and emotional bank account with one another? I asked which factors teachers believe are trust builders between teachers and principals. In addition, I asked whether principals' character or competence matters more to teachers. Additionally, I explored the influence of the length of time a teacher works for a principal from the perspective of trust building.

A Framework of Trust

Covey and Merrill (2006) say trust takes time to gain but takes no time to lose. Trust is expensive in terms of cost to a school or other organization when it is lost. Trust is a matter of confidence, and if the staff members in the school do not have confidence in the leader or the school, then distrust and suspicion will reign. Likewise, if staff members feel mistrust for one another, working together becomes more cumbersome. There are four core components of credibility: high integrity, good intent, excellent credentials, and a good track record. They believe the first two, high integrity and good intent, make up the construct of character. Good credentials and a good track record, on the other hand, make up the construct of competence. They theorize all four, or rather both competence and character, are necessary to build trust. In a time in which principals are being asked to evaluate teachers in such a way that impacts pay, tenure, etc., it is incredibly important that we achieve a balance of competence and character.

A Problem of Trust

The relationship between principal and teacher is a critical one to study if teachers are expected to collaborate with their administrators on issues of best teaching practices, teacher evaluations, parent relations, and student success. If teachers are expected to improve in their job performance, particularly if their compensation is going to be based on effective teaching practices and student achievement, educators and administrators must establish an effective working relationship. Since the principal of a school is the educational leader and, therefore, expected to model effective instructional strategies, good communication with parents, and positive student interactions, a relationship built on trust between principal and teacher must form. Trust within an organization such as a school aids in the success of the school and the stakeholders. Factor in the potential complications and new learning involved in the shift in teacher evaluation systems, and the necessity for trust is greatly increased.

It is, therefore, pertinent to examine the characteristics that foster the relationship of trust between principals and teachers as well as between staff members themselves. Since the sharing of best teaching practices has been shown to have a profound effect on teacher growth, it is incumbent upon school leaders to help foster a sense of trust within the school and between teachers.

Also, Covey and Merrill (2006) suggest in their theory of trust that character and competence have equal impact in determining teachers' trust in principals. However, I wonder if one element may be more significant than is the other. Equally important is determining if the length of time the principal and teacher have worked together impacts the level of trust. Other factors notwithstanding, does a teacher who has worked for a principal for 1 year trust his or her principal differently than the one working for a principal for 10 years? The ramifications will most assuredly influence the success of teacher observations and evaluations.

Leadership and School Reform

In response to the growing need for school reform because of the No Child Left Behind (NCLB) Act of 2001 (National Conference on State Legislatures, 2006), the role of the principal is changing and must continue to further evolve. School reform demands a culture of collaboration and relationships between school leaders and all stakeholders (Sergiovanni, 1995), and this collaboration will require building and maintaining relationships. Bryk and Schneider (2003) said trust will be the uniting feature for school reform and, therefore, is an important concept to study. I couldn't agree more. As much emphasis as we place on test scores, we should at least give that much credence to the aspect of trust in school settings.

R. Jones (2007) found a need for placing greater emphasis on leadership as a critical role for effectively changing how schools are led. Rothenberger (2008) found leadership behavior within an organization could be classified in terms of the power of relationships between leaders and employees. Leaders who remain in control by wielding their power over employees in the school will likely be viewed quite differently than leaders who gain the trust and mutual understanding of the stakeholders in the school. Margaret Thatcher once said, "Being powerful is like being a lady. If you have to tell people you are, you aren't." Shared leadership breeds shared relationships. Farmer (2010) said the importance of leadership behaviors was found to have a significant impact on teachers' attitudes toward teaching. Teachers were more likely to have better degrees of self-efficacy and intrinsic motivation when they perceived their principals to value core competencies such as reflection, inquiry, instructional leadership, and learning communities. Likewise, school leaders are more likely to be successful if they are working with staff members who are willing to trust each other and in their leadership.

Uses of This Text

While it is crucial to have a leader who is trustworthy, competent, and character filled, one person does not make or break the school culture. Staff members have an integral role in supporting one another and supporting the principal in the development of trust. Communication and honesty are critical for sharing concerns with grade level mates, other teachers in the department, between teachers and classroom assistants, and everyone else involved in the school. While much of my own trust research was based on teacher trust in the principal, I will spend time talking about how teachers can discover new ways to interact with one another to foster a maximum amount of trust. School leaders might use this book as a book study, stopping at regular intervals as well as at each "E-Cubed: Effective Evaluation Example" to consider their feelings and progress on each area of trust and communication. Each box is also designed to give a quick takeaway from the previous section or perhaps a little nugget of advice we can each use in our work starting immediately.

Defining Trust

Before we delve too deeply into trust, we must realize a true definition of trust needs to be established among stakeholders in a school. After all, how can we work toward something we haven't defined? Tschannen-Moran (1998) defined trust as the willingness to be vulnerable to another person who is open, honest, reliable, and competent. Trust can also be described as having an emotional bank account with another person. The account is available for deposits that occur when someone does something that adds to the trust between the two people. In talking to educators and school leaders across the country, I have come to define trust as *the ease with which we believe in, rely on, and have faith in the idea that the other person is going to do what he or she says.* And, the proof is in the pudding. One cannot simply say they will do something or that they believe a certain way. We will truly trust when we see the person actually walking the walk, not just talking the talk. When trust is present in relationships, communication is made easier, on all levels. We feel more comfortable in opening up and showing a bit of vulnerability. Take the classic example of a breakup in a relationship. After such a breakup, one might find it difficult to open up or share themselves with another person. Much like a flower that seems reluctant to open its petals or a turtle too shy to stick its head out of the safety of a shell, we may have learned and evolved to be cautious in opening up to others after being hurt. But, little by little, if we are willing to dip just one little tippy-tippy toe into the water of vulnerability to another person, we often find the water becomes warmer and safer as we go. Take the examples, below, of dipping toes in the water of trust.

> "My principal made my day today. He supported me, totally, in a very difficult parent conference."

> "One of the teachers in our school came to me to discuss a concern instead of taking it directly to the teacher's union. I think she believes we can work it out together."

> "My grade level mates and I disagreed on the appropriate way to handle a curriculum issue, but we all agreed to disagree, and it all worked out in a win-win fashion."

These are all actual examples of trust, expressed from teachers and principals in schools across the country.

One of the premises of the emotional bank account is the recognition that at some point in every relationship, we are going to make a withdrawal. In other words, at some point, we are going to mess up in our communication, honesty, or support. When that happens, if we have enough deposits, there is no reason our relationship should go into the red and be completely overdrawn. We may have to make a few more trust deposits before feeling our relationship is back to normal, but the overall trust shouldn't be jeopardized if the bulk of the account has been based on deposits. It is important to know which actions, behaviors, and characteristics make up a holistic approach to trust. Schools can start by having a group conscience, in which everyone is allowed and invited to contribute to what defines trust for them. Finding a common definition of trust is quite likely to spur the school staff into getting on the same page.

A great starting place is to ask: *If our school was the illustration for the definition of trust, what would people see (hear, feel) when they walked through the doors of our school?* Once those actions, behaviors, and characteristics are named, then staff members can begin exploring what strategies will help to achieve that point. For example, if most everyone includes the action of "telling the truth, even if it's difficult to hear," which many respondents to my surveys said, then the group can begin to build in strategies to encourage that behavior. One strategy schools have found helpful to encourage telling the truth, no matter what, is to share success stories of when this has paid off.

For example, when I was a guidance counselor and taught lessons on character education in every elementary classroom, we would always talk about honesty. Someone would always say something like, "But if I tell the truth that I broke the lamp in the living room, I'm going to get in trouble," to which I would do my level best *not* to reply. Instead, I would invite comments from other students in the class. Inevitably, several students would have good news stories that ended in, "My mom wasn't happy, but she said since I was honest, she wasn't going to punish me." Some savvy student would likely even say something like, "Even if you have to deal with the consequences, you can still sleep at night because you did the right thing."

A school is the ultimate example of a system at work. While my study focused mainly on what teachers said they needed in order to trust in the administrator, staff relationships play a pivotal role in the way a school is able to function. In other words, a good school climate may start with a good leader, but everyone has a role to play in this system. In a marriage, husbands need to do things to make marriage better. Wives need to do things to make marriage better. But systemically, if everyone is not at least on the same sheet of music, the marriage is not likely to last past the end of the song.

In a school system, when leaders and staff members are not on the same page, every effort to make the culture better in schools will be made monumentally more difficult. When communication, honesty, and support are present, the school becomes a second home and an enjoyable haven to come to every day. In essence, the system feeds itself into a safe, healthy, and more content loop. And a trusting system is what is necessary for successful implementation of the teacher evaluation process.

Since relationships and trust between principals and teachers are fundamental components of the operations of schools (Bryk & Schneider, 2002), it is incumbent upon school leaders to determine what level of trust exists in schools and to work to improve the current level of trust. The study on trust between principals and teachers (Arneson, 2012) allowed me to determine if competence or character plays a larger role in the determination of overall trust teachers perceive in principals. In addition, I solicited teacher input about the principal behaviors teachers feel most determine the level of trust they feel for the principal. The resulting behaviors were then categorized into themes. These behaviors were compiled into a list of best practices for administrative leadership classes and for principals new to the field to learn what builds trust. Seasoned administrators feeling the growing pains of a new evaluation system will benefit greatly by hearing from teachers what is likely to build trust. This list was expanded to include what teachers and other staff members can do to improve trust in their school. The best practices are the strategies that encompass the remainder of the book, allowing principals and teachers a firsthand look at what is needed in order to trust, particularly in the area of observations and evaluations, and the steps they can take to get there.

This book calls us to address the elephant in the room. The elephant in the room is the thing everyone recognizes, but no one wants to admit is a problem, for fear it might cause too much tension to address it. The irony is everyone is likely talking about the elephant in the room to their close friends and family members (i.e., "No one at my school trusts one another" or "We feel like we are always the last to know" or "Our principal is really sweet, but I'm not sure I can trust he's doing the best things for me to grow, professionally."),

People are just often extremely nervous about addressing the elephant head on, preferring instead to talk about the issues as if they aren't staring us straight in the face.

In fact, we not only must acknowledge and address the elephant, we must also engage the elephant. Let's address the tension and not ignore it. Miscommunication is one of the elephants in the room—it gets in the way of teacher evaluations, progress on professional goals, and a safe morale-filled environment in which to work. How often have you encountered good educators who would be willing to be more reflective on their teaching practice, if only they felt a sense of comfort with their coach, mentor, and yes, even the principal?

We can engage the elephant and make evaluations and the inner workings of a school environment much more pleasant by highlighting strategies for better communication, honesty, and support.

SOLUTIONS

I recently read a quote that says, "Speak in such a way that others love to listen to you. Listen in such a way that others love to speak to you." What a two-way-street way to look at communication. This is what communication and relationships are all about, right? I believe, in my heart, we all want this type of synchronous relationship with those with and for whom we work. The solutions and strategies proposed in this book are based soundly on this belief that we can improve communication if we simply value it and nurture it.

Some of the strategies might appear to be based on common sense. In fact, that may be partly true, but the strategies are also based on research that allowed teachers to voice their opinions about what they needed in order to be fully committed to this evaluation system that, in many cases, is the impetus for teacher pay and bonuses. Communication and trust will be the cornerstones to the success of such a new system.

CHAPTER TWO

Evaluations Done "With" Teachers, Not "to" Teachers

If you give respect, you'll get respect. The same goes for loyalty, and trust and all the other virtues that I believe great leaders have to offer.

> —John Wooden, Legendary UCLA Basketball Coach

During my first year of teaching students with emotional disturbances in San Antonio, Texas, I was told one day that I would be observed the next week. "Get out a good lesson," one of the veteran teachers in my building told me. "Who will observe me? What are they looking for?" I asked. Without clear-cut answers, I decided I should just do what I had been doing in my classroom for the last several weeks. After all, my students were doing well, behaviorally, and they were actually turned on to reading (a first for many of them). All I knew is I wouldn't know the person doing the observation, and they would give me their notes when they were finished. To say I felt a lack of control would be the understatement of the century.

The day of my observation came. I told my kids we would be having a visitor in our classroom (I had learned that surprises didn't bode too well with my students) who would be seeing how I teach and how they learn. At 10:00, a gentleman walked in, sat down at an extra desk and took notes for about 30 minutes, then got up and left the room. The next day, I found a three-page pink copy of a triplicate report in my mailbox. I opened it and read the notes the observer had collected, including "Great job keeping the students under control" and "You shouldn't give a break in the middle of a lesson." While I was thrilled with a high score on the overall evaluation, I asked my principal when I would meet with the observer. He shook his head. "I don't think you meet with the observer. He just does the evaluation." So noted. Evaluation done "to" me. How I yearned, in that first year of teaching, to talk to someone about my decisions in teaching. And what of this "control" of the kids?

That was in 1988, and I wish I could say that antiquated form of observation and evaluation is blasé now. However, talks with teachers and administrators across the country indicate otherwise. In fact, teachers with whom I speak say they often are called to the office by the secretary to "sign off" on their evaluations and then given a copy of the report. And yet, as a principal, I had teachers who clamored for more feedback. "Did you see that the new table arrangement encouraged better discussion between students?" they asked. "What are some ways I can increase student participation through the use of whiteboards?" they asked me.

We hear it said that teaching is like living on an island. If this is the case, my suggestion is to provide ferry service between these isolated land masses. In many cases, the administrator can act as the ferry operator, providing the access needed for teachers to share best practices with one another. After all, who better than someone who is able to visit lots of classrooms to provide insight and feedback to teachers? One of my favorite parts about being a school administrator was having the ability and privilege of seeing effective teaching strategies in place and then sharing those strategies when another teacher was in need. For example, I go and watch Mrs. R teach a writing lesson, complete with students sharing examples of well-written metaphors with each other. When I visit Mr. P's class, he asks afterwards if I know of any resources to help reluctant writers share. I can either name some strategies I saw in Mrs. R's class or, better yet, refer Mr. P to Mrs. R. Poof! Ferry crossing complete. Better yet, we may have just established a bit of professional learning community along the way. The caution, of course, is to make certain Mrs. R is not always the go-to teacher. The best collaborative learning I have witnessed is when educators regard each other as learners and not the end-all-be-all experts.

E-Cubed: Effective Evaluation Example

Share best practices viewed during observations
with other teachers in need of similar strategies.

In the same fashion, school leaders need to model this same type of willingness to admit mistakes or admit we don't know it all in order to establish a culture of mutual respect. If school leaders always appear to have it all together in front of the staff, many will think this unrealistic and furthermore not wish to show vulnerability in front of someone who "never errs." One way to demonstrate this is in faculty meetings or professional development opportunities. As I teach workshops on the Danielson framework for teaching, I am citing examples throughout the trainings of effective routines and procedures. If I misplace something, I might say, "This is NOT an example of a distinguished 2c (or way of managing my materials)." If I ask a question then answer it myself, I might point out I need to work on my questioning techniques a bit more. In other words, nobody is perfect. Everyone knows nobody is perfect. However, it is nice for the school leader to admit he or she is not above reproach and, furthermore, to talk about ways to improve for next time.

In my book *Communicate and Motivate* (Arneson, 2011a), I talk about how we can talk with each other in such a way that is neither offensive nor hurtful. It is, after all, not always what we say but how we say it that makes all the difference between appreciation and resentment. We all have examples that come to mind—customer service representatives who say, "No, we can't do that" instead of "Let me see what I can do." In the classroom, I learned how to say, "Make sure you clean up your desk as quickly as possible so we can get to recess on time" instead of "We're not going anywhere until this mess is cleaned up."

Words have such great power. They have the power to direct, destroy, and delight. When I was a guidance counselor in an elementary school, I taught character-building lessons in the classroom, some on how to handle peer pressure and bullying. We talked about the old adage "Sticks and stones may break your bones but words will never hurt you." I'd ask if students believed this was true. Some would say, "I can decide whether or not I'm going to let somebody's mean words hurt me." Very true, and I always like to complement those students who are truly able to do that.

I believe, however, those folks are few and far between, because letting go of someone's hurtful words takes a pretty highly evolved self-esteem. In those lessons, inevitably, some wise and tender-hearted soul would pipe up, "But words *can* be hurtful." Absolutely!! Words can destroy relationships, for sure. We've all been on one end or the other of this phenomenon. We have but to look at examples of people who have taken their own lives and left notes and letters saying, "I just couldn't take hearing the words of the bullies and tormentors anymore."

But words can also delight and heal. I used to teach a lesson on caring, in which the students in the class would all write one sincere compliment to a particular student. The looks on the faces of those who read their compliments, either out loud or to themselves, were priceless. Furthermore, the power of giving an accolade to someone can be extremely powerful and delightful as well. When I was a principal, and parents or community members would come in the school and give kudos to the school, the staff, or a particular teacher, I would tell them I was going to immediately and assuredly pass the news along to the person being revered. I would then thank the person who brought the good news, saying, "It's one thing to think a thing like 'I was really impressed with the way she handled that conference' but a wholly other thing to take time out of one's day, sometimes making a special trip, to say it out loud." I would thank them for taking that extra step in the compliment cycle. Certainly, we don't want to operate solely on the basis of approval seeking, but words from other folks matter to us, as we are social beings.

Words can also direct us and guide us in becoming better educators and better people. As a principal, I suggest giving specific feedback on teacher observations, such as "How can you add more higher-order questions to your lessons?" Worded differently, the same feedback could sound like "You asked WAY too many rote questions." Words can, then, act as a rudder, directing the boat of the conversation or even relationship. I have often said, "It's not what we say; it's how we say it" (2011a). In other words, the steering of the boat is impacted by sometimes very subtle changes in the handling of the oars or wheel. We should be aware that our words carry the power to direct and guide and make the best use of our tone of voice, word choice, and semantics.

Mr. W came to our school from another neighboring school. He said he had been told, at his previous school, that he had horrible grammar skills. "You can't teach fifth graders if you can't speak correctly" had been the admonishment. While he had some habits that needed breaking, we saw the potential for great connections with students. Instead of "dinging" him for every grammar error, we suggested he have a jar in his room in which he would put in a marble if the students "caught" him in a grammar error. A full marble jar would result in a popcorn party. A true win-win in everyone's book, we felt, as it encouraged the students to use what they were learning but also held Mr. W accountable for learning, modeling, and correcting. His willingness to tackle such a potential problem was icing on the cake.

E-Cubed: Effective Evaluation Example

Give specific feedback in such a way that it feels "shared" versus being "told to" the teacher.

While not every district requires post-observation conferences, I believe it is without a doubt one of the most important practices in which a teacher and principal can participate. After all, in the case of my first year of teaching, a post-observation conference might have allowed me to get some learning-focused feedback from my observer and might have given me the chance to tell him about the workshop I had just attended that taught us a research-based practice for giving students with emotional disabilities a break every 30 minutes. Simply being allowed to explain and explore my own thinking about my teaching practice would have been so incredibly empowering. I know this from being a part of some highly enlightening conferences myself.

What resonates most for me about the practice of conducting post-observation conferences is the power of the conversation that ensues. Consider, for example, the teacher who asks 18 questions during her lesson on mathematical arrays, but 15 questions are yes/no questions and only directed to students in the front half of the class. Just being able to review that data with an observer has the potential for an incredible learning opportunity. "I had no idea I wasn't calling on students in the back half of the room. And as for my questions, I am starting to write several higher-order questions on sticky notes to put on my lesson plan so I don't forget." Isn't the ultimate goal of a reflective conversation to reflect on practice and possibly add some new tools to our teaching toolkit that will impact student growth?

If we are going to engage in reflective conversations at the conclusion of an observation, there are several preliminary steps that must be in place.

1. The culture of trust must be established in advance

A collaborative effort to build communication is a great start. We need to begin with the end in mind. We need to have a good idea of where we are headed in order to make good progress toward that goal each day. In other words, we should ask the question: What would our school look and sound like if we had a collective culture of good communication? Whatever you, collectively, say you would like it to look and sound like is the end. Begin with that as a goal and work toward it. If, for example, you say, "We want everyone in the school—from students to parents to staff—to greet each other with a good morning greeting each day," then expect it from everyone. Start simply by issuing a challenge to staff to see how many people they can greet each morning. Might people make fun of this practice at first? Sure, but they will be doing it all the same.

The culture of trust will go a long way toward making the evaluation process done "with" teachers more collaborative and palatable.

2. The invitation to mutually participate must be present

Laura Lipton and Bruce Wellman (2013) talk at length about the power of the inviting introduction to a conversation. Beginning a post-observation conference with "Here's what you did well and here's what you need to do differently next time" is so limiting. Telling shuts down thinking and turns people off. Instead, why not begin the conversation with an open-ended question? For example, "What are some thoughts you are having about the lesson?" invites participation with the teacher. If a culture of trust has been established, teachers will open up about their reflection on the lesson. The key is for administrators to not use the vulnerability of the teacher against them. If, for example, a teacher reflects that his students with disabilities were not as engaged as he had hoped, it would be completely unfair for the administrator to go and mark the teacher down on the evaluation form on engagement. On the contrary, the teacher then should be praised for his willingness to explore areas for growth.

3. The conversation must focus on the data, not the personalities

In workshops I teach on effective communication, I often ask teachers if they can teach a student they do not particularly like. Likewise, I ask administrators if they can evaluate teachers for whom there is little love lost. There is usually a titter of nervous laughter, because, frankly, we've all been there. But inevitably, the answer comes out, "I may not like it, but I have to do it."

Years ago, I worked with a teacher who rubbed many staff members the wrong way. Her negativity was baffling to an otherwise super-positive staff. I might even admit to a bit of bias the first time I went to observe her in action. "She can't possibly show respect to her students with the way she treats the rest of the world" might have been a thought that went through my head. Lo and behold, when I began taking notes during a walkthrough, I saw just the opposite. Encouraging words to her students were the norm, not the exception. In a post-observation conference, the data points were shared (along with a question, "How might you expand your encouragement of students to encouragement of fellow staff members?")

Collaborative conversations, if done correctly, have the capacity to encourage growth in teachers far beyond the one lesson upon which a post-observation conference is based. For example, consider the difference between the two following questions:

a. If you taught this lesson again, how would you group your students differently?
b. What are some of your guiding thoughts about grouping your students?

While the first may be more specific, the second encourages the feeling of growth and opportunity. The first suggests the observer believes the teacher should have grouped students differently, possibly putting the teacher on the defense.

When first attempted, the collaborative nature of a conversation may be a bit difficult. For example, a teacher new to my school
looked at me with a deer-in-the-headlights look when I invited her to
talk about her thinking surrounding a reading strategy she had used
in her lesson. "Oops, I thought you were going to tell me how I did
on my observation," she apologized when she fumbled for words
to explain her thinking. "Nobody has ever asked me any questions.
My last principal would just say 'Looked great' and ask me to sign
the paper." I sympathized totally, as the same practice had been used
with me for so long, and I allowed her the time she needed to formu-
late her response.

The lesson I learned was: Just because it's the right thing to do
doesn't mean it is going to be easy. The paradigm shift to collaboration is truly a process, one not to be taken lightly. It is, however, a
process that is well worth the effort. My best analogy to this is the
time and energy it takes to "train" a new class of Kindergarteners
in the expectations and procedures you expect in the class. It takes
time (and patience and meditation and. . . .) to teach 4- and 5-year
olds how you want them to line up according to table groups or how
to pass their papers to the front of the class. But, wowee, is the pain
worth the gain once the culture is in place? Same holds true for the
culture of promoting one's own learning in reflection conversations.
Laying the groundwork takes time, to be sure, but the benefits are
reaped heartily when teachers begin popping in your office to say,
"Hey, just wanted you to know I am going to Jil's room after school
today to get some more tips on how she runs her math groups" or
"The next time you do a walkthrough in my class, watch how the
kids are taking ownership of their supply boxes on their tables."

And, by the way, for schools in which post-observation conferences are not required, teachers can still be advocates for their need
for feedback and growth. One teacher in New York shared that even
though post-observation conferences weren't required, she would
seek out her assistant principal after an observation and ask for a
conversation anyway. "I didn't want to put him on the spot" she told
me, "but I needed some help." She said she also recognized that the
way in which she asked for the conference made all the difference in
the world. "If I would have said, 'You need to meet with me,' I might
have made him mad. As it was, I said I would love to talk about my
discipline strategies with him. In the end, he was able to make some
suggestions I hadn't thought about before."

It is important to note that feedback with teachers doesn't just have to be done with the administrator. Other options for reflection partners include grade-level mates, other teachers in the department, or even help from online sources. At my former elementary school, one grade level had such a high level of trust with one another, they would all bring their copies of their evaluations to a grade-level meeting, share the feedback, and offer support in the areas of growth for each teacher. "I saw a great website for using question prompts," "Deb uses a graphic organizer that might help with that," and "One of the things that helped me with that was going back to Harry Wong's (2004) book *The First Days of School*" were comments heard among this community of learners, whose premise remained helping each other as the best kind of help.

Being willing to be vulnerable and being willing to admit we don't have all the answers is the key to such a collaborative culture.

If, indeed, the ultimate goal of the observation and evaluation process is to grow as a learner in order to grow as a teacher, then the shift simply must take place from evaluation done "to" teachers to evaluations done "with" teachers. People will not care how much you know until they know how much you care.

CHAPTER THREE

Building Teacher Trust and Communication in the Evaluation Process

Assumptions are the termites of relationships.

—Henry Winkler

After reading anecdotal comments from teachers about what behaviors, actions, and characteristics of a principal increased trust, it became clear that communication is the frontrunner of all. Communication ranked even higher than honesty in categories of behaviors that built trust in the principal. But how could that be? Isn't honesty the number one factor in building trust? How can one trust another if honesty is not present? Perhaps in many cases, honesty was assumed, but teachers referred to open communication more often than honesty as a major trust builder.

WHAT THE RESEARCH SAYS ABOUT TRUST

The literature about leaders is full of studies suggesting the same thing. Turner (2010) suggests communication is a cooperative process between two individuals with an exchange and sequence of thoughts, feelings, or ideas toward a mutual goal or direction. Communication can considerably improve trust when leaders choose to be open with employees. Conversely, Turner said employees can be incredibly resentful when management remains silent as rumors surface.

Trust is cited in areas such as communication and leadership inextricably (Mayer, Davis, & Schoorman, 1995), indicating good leadership may be because of good communication, or perhaps good communication between leaders and employees comes from effective leadership. Effective leadership is simply a must-have when it comes to an evaluation process done with teachers and not to teachers. Noddings (2005) said that a fundamental component of caring is open-ended communication, allowing for both parties to speak, both parties to listen, and neither party knowing from the outset the end result of the conversation. The open-ended nature of communication is particularly important between teachers and principals, as teachers need to feel the direction of the conversation with the principal is not already predetermined.

Communicating expectations and information pertinent to job completion is also important to trust, as Reina and Reina (2006) point out the importance of giving employees the information they need to do their jobs. Teachers want to know where they stand and how to get better in their teaching and classroom management strategies. Several behaviors related to trust, such as allowing people to make decisions, seeking others' input, and helping other people learn skills are crucial as well. Bies and Tripp (1996) identify actions that violate trust, including violating the rules, changing the rules after the fact, breaking promises, stealing of ideas, criticizing, and accusing of unfair treatment. Many of these trust barriers include inappropriate or ill-fated communication.

In McGregor's (1960) book about the human side of business, he says mutual trust is intricately intertwined with good communication. As a social psychologist, McGregor did extensive research about relationships and interactions in the workplace. Without open communication, McGregor posits, trust will be severely limited and likewise, without trust, open communication will be next to impossible. Regarding communication, a further question to explore is whether trust impacts communication more or communication impacts trust more.

Hall (2006) researched trust-building behaviors of a middle school principal, and certain behaviors were identified prominently in promoting trust and relationships with teachers in the school. One of the main categories of behaviors was found to be in the communicative category, including openness, credibility, visibility, and confidentiality. Brimhall (2010) studied the lack of trust between faculty and principal, faculty and client, and faculty and colleague in secondary schools. Brimhall conducted a quantitative study to determine the relationship between administrative communicator styles and level of perceived trust. Respondents completed the Communicator Style Measure and the Omnibus Trust Scale. Brimhall found a relationship between communicator styles and trust levels for principals. Specifically, Brimhall found a significant difference among communicator styles in terms of influence on trust for principals and colleagues.

Communication increases trust. Turner (2010) said good communication instilled trust in leaders because communication and trust allow the employees in organizations to offer input without feeling inferior to the leaders in the school. While there is an inherent power differential between leaders of the school and the teachers employed therein, the difference need not imply one role is less important than the other. Particularly regarding a growth model for teaching performance, a more level playing field proves to be much more collaborative than a one-sided or top-down model.

Turner (2010) said the investigation of the relationship between trust behaviors of leaders and the organizational trust perceived by employees can play a key role for other organizations undergoing change. Information gleaned from one study could impact the training and hiring practices in organizations across the country. Kagy (2010) purported to find which behaviors of principals either promoted or hindered trust based on the insights of 21 teachers.

How was communication manifested in my own research? Although many teachers simply wrote they wanted a principal who was a good communicator, others were more specific. Some anecdotal comments included: "The principal talks to us openly," "He has an open door policy," and "She makes time to talk to us." Looking at the antithesis of this is equally vital. Barriers to good communication included the following:

1. Letting employees be the last to know

2. Not responding to emails or phone calls

3. Lack of open or effective communication

4. Closed doors

5. Not listening and other poor communication skills

In Chapter 9, we'll delve more deeply into the top five.

1. *Letting employees be the last to know:* Administrators need to be proactive in getting information to teachers before they find it out elsewhere. This particularly includes information about the evaluation process and observation cycle required by the district or state.

2. *Not responding to emails or phone calls:* Timely feedback is crucial in the evaluation process but can be manifested in many different ways.

3. *Lack of open or effective communication:* Teachers express concern about the lack of good communication and, many times, even expressed concern that the principal may be unable to communicate effectively. Effective communication is a must-have when it comes to trust in the evaluation process.

4. *Closed doors:* Particularly in the time of change, teachers need to know that the principal's door is always open for questions and concerns.

5. *Not listening and other poor communication skills:* A dear friend recently gave me a sweatshirt that says, "Silent and Listen have the same letters. Coincidence? I don't think so." We need to be fully prepared to listen to the concerns of others if we are going to make strides toward increasing trust and communication.

STRATEGIES FOR BUILDING BETTER COMMUNICATION

If principals are going to be trusted by teachers based on their communication skills, what specific skills will this require?

1. Open door policy

Teachers shared frustrations with principals who "hid in the office." This is certainly true of any job and of any leader. Anyone in a leadership role needs to show their face to the crowd in order to role model. Principals must be present and communicate vision to all stakeholders, first and foremost, or else risk distrust and mistrust. Particularly in the first year of teacher evaluation implementation, our teachers had a zillion questions. They needed to know the door was open to come in and say, "This scares me." Or "How can I get better at this?" Admittedly, administrators will likely say they enjoy this part of their job but can't seem to find the time amidst all the other work of the day: Paperwork that must get done, budgets that don't ever seem to balance, angry parents who must see you immediately, not to mention children who are making poor choices and need to be counseled on the right way to behave in the lunchroom or on the bus. But making time to have that open door policy is the first step to a communicative relationship that builds trust. Mark Shellenger is the project director for the national School Administration Manager (SAM) Project. SAM helps principals understand how they use their time, gives them a staff person (the "SAM") to whom operations responsibilities are delegated, and provides them with strategies for what to do with their newly found time to lead efforts to improve instruction in the school.

And what will kill trust quicker than a flyswatter knocks down the pesky fly is an administrator who tries to tell teachers how busy they are. "I can't talk to you right now. I have 400 phone messages to return and I haven't even eaten lunch." NO!! Any of us who have been in the classroom for any length of time know how busy it is to plan lessons, gather materials, confer with other teachers, contact parents, and enter grades. And that is all in addition to the day's work of teaching the children in the classroom. The last thing teachers want to hear is how busy principals are. We need to make the time for important and worthwhile conversations. And let's face the facts: What could be more important than improving professional teaching practices among the educators with whom we work?

E-Cubed: Effective Evaluation Example

"I am looking forward to talking with you about ways
you can improve your questioning techniques.
How about we set up a time for this afternoon or
tomorrow when we won't be rushed?"

2. Address the elephant in the room

Too often, in any difficult conversation, we act as if we don't notice the signs of discomfort from the other person. When the elephant appears, it often looks like this:

The principal asks the teacher how they would change the lesson that was just observed. The teacher dances around the issue, fearful that any sign of vulnerability will be misconstrued as weakness as a teacher. In other words, the teacher is thinking, "I don't want to admit any of my mistakes lest you decide to change your 'rating' of me to something lower." "Don't admit defeat!" seems to be the underlying battle cry. All the while, the principal is probably sitting across the desk (we'll talk about room arrangement later on), thinking, "Hey, if you want any sort of good evaluation, you better admit you did something wrong or I will assume you don't know how to be reflective about your teaching." Notice that all this is *not said*. It is, instead, thought. The call to action, in this case, is for someone to address the elephant in the room. We must acknowledge the fear of the teacher to express what he or she might perceive as weakness and say, "I get it that you fear if you share a way you could have improved the lesson, you think I will have fodder to lower your rating. But we need to trust this process and part of the process is being reflective on the teaching. Talking about ways the lesson could have been improved is a great example of growth." Or, better yet, ask the teacher how he or she is feeling. I like to know how teachers perceive actively searching for ways to improve their teaching. If they see it as admitting defeat, Houston, we have a problem. We administrators, as instructional leaders, need to ensure there is not a shred of truth to that fear. Looking for ways to hone one's craft, in my opinion, is a true indicator of teacher professionalism and growth, and must be treated as such.

3. It's not what you say; it's how you say it

While training teachers on how to build respect and rapport in the classroom, I had assigned a reading assignment to jigsaw. Each teacher had 10 minutes to skim and highlight their own passage before expertly teaching the other members of their table group (who had, in true jigsaw fashion, been assigned their own reading passages). I started the timer, and silent reading time began. One table group was explaining the assignment to a member who had just returned from a break, when one teacher at another table called out, "Hey, so what part of silent reading do you all not get? Why doesn't everyone just shut up now?" Wowee! How about the irony that the reading passage was about respect and rapport? I quietly said, "And just like in the classroom, when we want our students to be respectful to one another, we need to make sure if it is silent reading time and someone is talking out loud, we can say something like, 'It may just be me, but I concentrate so much better when everyone reads silently.'" Clearly, we both tried to convey the same message, which was "Be quiet for silent reading," but the way it was said the first time caused massive dissention in the ranks. We always have a choice to think about how we will say something and make the decision to say it in such a way that it will be heard and not lost to its negativity.

E-Cubed: Effective Evaluation Example

Instead of saying, "I think you could have improved the lesson by grouping your students differently," why not try, "How might different student groups make a difference in the learning?"

---

4. Do you want to be right or do you want for the relationship to be alright?

Active listening inherently means we are engaged in an active exchange of thoughts and ideas, not simply a one-sided diatribe. Nowhere is this truer than in communication between teachers and principals. Likely due to the already evident power differential between the two roles, sometimes the power difference is perpetuated by the communication style or strategy by the administrator. An effective point to keep in mind is listening actively without fast-forwarding to "As soon as this teacher is finished talking, I'll tell her how it really is."

Just ask any marriage counselor, who will likely tell you divorce is predicated on this exact problem. Whether it is an evolved tactic, or one that was present at the time of matrimony and ultimately nurtured to the point of no return, when spouses only listen to one another with half an ear while they wait impatiently to teach the other spouse "a lesson," it is harmful and poisonous. We have to make a commitment to making things alright versus always wanting to simply be right.

5. Three kisses and a wish

A great teaching strategy my dear friend Angelle uses in her classroom is "three kisses and a wish." While she uses it for students to give each other feedback in the writing process in her 2nd grade classroom, I advocate the use of it in post-observation teacher/principal conferences. It is just what it says without the actual osculation. A principal tells a teacher, "I saw several instances of higher-order questioning in your lesson today" and continues with two other good news items before delving into constructive criticism. The premise, of course, is if you lose your audience with negativity from the outset, you might as well finish your comments talking to a stump. The negative comments have a sneaky way of building up a wall between principal and teacher. You can almost visibly see the wall rise up from the floor and harm any further effective communication. Starting off with a positive piece of evidence will likely keep the options open for communication and ultimately for learning and growth.

CHAPTER FOUR

Builder 1

Build Relationships, Not an Empire

I never understood why Clark Kent was so hell bent on keeping Lois Lane in the dark.

—Audrey Niffenegger,
The Time Traveler's Wife

With all the legislative mandates, administrators have a great deal to manage in a school. From the pressure to manage a balanced budget to hiring quality employees to addressing parent concerns about the safety of their children, the administrative job is one filled with pressure. Couple this with the more recent development of high-stakes testing and resulting high-stakes teacher evaluation, and the consequences can be devastating. Shortcuts to good quality relationships are often the result. Covey (1989) believed emotional bank accounts between people are built with every single exchange. If that is true, and I vehemently believe it is, administrators can't afford to take any conversations with teachers lightly. In other words, every time administrators speak publicly or privately to teachers, there is the potential for a trust building or trust barrier scenario. What makes it or breaks it?

1. *Time:* This means we make the time to talk, not wedge a conversation in to an already frenetically crazy day. When trying to schedule a potentially difficult conversation regarding an observation

that had not gone as well as the teacher had hoped, the teacher asked, "Could we wait until after school to meet? I am afraid I will get emotional about what happened, and I don't want to go into my classroom and face my students in that state." Although it might have been much more convenient to meet then, it was important to respect the request for time.

2. *Openness:* This means recognizing, as an administrator, the conversation is not all about us. If I am only listening to the teacher with half an ear because I am lying in wait to "pounce" with my own agenda, the teacher will finally simply succumb and endure. The question we must ask ourselves is, What is the most effective method of communicating such that the outcome is true teacher growth in areas the administrator and teacher agree will most impact student learning?

3. *Willingness:* The willingness is apparent in our ability as administrators to show a little bit of vulnerability, to not try to come across as "the keepers of the knowledge." If we are willing to show a bit of admission that we might not have all the answers, teachers often paradoxically believe we have a great bit of wisdom to share. How different is this than the parent who lectures and lectures their child on the dangers of driving while texting, only to have the biggest impact occur after a "text-while-driving" conversation comes up organically from the child? Willingness is often the first step in building the trusting relationship.

What is your true purpose and motivation in saying what you say? We must examine this question in an honest way. Dr. McEachern, the assistant superintendent when I was hired to be a principal, gave me some of the best advice of my career. He said to keep the child at the center of every decision I made as an administrator. He suggested that although conversations with parents and teachers would always need to occur, we couldn't ever go wrong if we kept the child in the center of the conversation.

Remaining in empire protection mode often is a result of fear on the administrator's part: fear of not looking competent, fear of not getting all the work done in a satisfactory fashion, and/or fear of lack of respect from teachers. The irony is, of course, that when we quit trying to control people and reactions and begin to trust the process a bit more, the respect we were fearing we would lose is actually increased. This is what I call the paradox of letting go. This does not mean, for an instant, that we let go of the process completely; it simply means we don't have to hang on like we are in a fight for our lives. The best analogy I can think of is riding a horse. When the rider is so tense and anxious about staying in control, he often tightens his legs around the horse's midsection, giving unintentional signals to the horse. In the same fashion, the novice rider often holds so tightly to the reins, the horse gets confused and anxious about the motives of the rider. If, instead, the rider can let up a little and trust the process, all the while remaining in a position of confidence and control, the ride becomes pleasant at the very least.

A counseling professor at New Mexico State University, Rod Merta, who taught me a good bit about what I know about counseling, used to tell us, "Trust the process." All that meant to me at the time is to be aware, as a counseling intern, I wasn't micromanaging the counseling session. As an administrator trying to coach teachers in professional practice, my view of trusting the process has expanded a good deal.

Trusting others to show off their own abilities without telling them exactly how to do it has profound implications. My husband and I learned early on with our first Labrador Retriever puppy, K.C., that she was desperate for the boundaries, rules, and policies of our household. However, she was a smart little girl, and she also wanted to believe we trusted her to be a big girl and make good choices. While we had friends who said their Lab would literally bolt from the front yard if taken off leash, K.C. thrived on it. With just a little bit of freedom at first, complete with coaching on our part ("Whoops! Too far, K.C. come this way!" accompanied by a quick tug on her leash), she learned her boundaries, while also learning a new and sophisticated skill— fetching the paper. Freedom in the process coupled with coaching and guidance proved to be the perfect combination for maximum learning. K.C. passed away at age 11, but her legacy lives on with us (Arneson, 2011b). Every Lab we have raised since then never bolts from the yard and respects the coaching and love she gets with Mom and Dad.

E-Cubed: Effective Evaluation Example

"I don't need to micromanage every single exchange in order to have effective conversations with my teachers." How is this statement manifested in your own leadership style?

In speaking with teachers all over the country about teacher evaluation and the new legislative emphasis on pay for performance, I hear the fear on the teachers' parts. Their fear stems primarily from not knowing whether or not they can trust their principals. In some cases, there is no question—the relationship between teacher and principal has been soured so detrimentally, it is irreparable. Teacher tenure and pay for performance are now often dependent upon one or two observations by an administrator, sometimes coupled with test scores and sometimes student surveys. The Measures of Effective Teaching project that was a research partnership between 3000 volunteer teachers and many research partners, concluded that an end-of-year score for a teacher can be based on several different models of percentages assigned to each of the above factors, depending on the state. Teachers are often anxious because they feel so much of those factors are out of their control, but first and foremost, they worry that the administrator evaluation piece will not be fair or equitable if trust does not exist between teacher and administrator. Instead of getting defensive about the teacher's fear, the administrator can convey understanding and work toward a better relationship.

While conducting a recent training, the group and I were discussing a teacher video we had just watched. The learning goal was to assign a level of performance to the teacher's ability to establish rapport with and among the class. One administrator started shaking her head and blurted out, "When are we going to get to talk about how this lesson sucked?" After I picked my jaw up off the floor, I reiterated the goal of this particular task. "Just a reminder. . . . We are only talking about the evidence we collected about respect and rapport from this particular video." The administrator started waving her hand, saying, "Oh sure, he might have been nice to his kids but the lesson sucked!" I will be honest. I felt heat rise up my neck. All I could think is, "I do not want this administrator to be evaluating any teachers in this school, district, or even country with that attitude." The premise, of course, is that she believes she needs to be blunt with teachers in telling them they "suck," even if parts of the teacher practice are clearly at a high level of performance. "They might not want to hear it," she reasoned, "but they need to hear they stink!"

There are a myriad of problems with this particular attitude, not the least of which the teacher this administrator "coaches" will never hear the message of what he or she needs to improve for being so busy building a defense against the way the message is sent. We have the great capacity to ignore a message if we believe the messenger is either evil or insane. So, to what end is the principal sending their caustic message?

Instead, I propose we need to simply do what Thumper's mother told him to do. Think before you speak. The relationship between administrator and teacher has the potential to be precarious at best. With the negative tone of "advice giving" in the above example, the relationship doesn't stand a chance.

Consider this teaching. The principal has just observed a lesson in which the teacher establishes respect and rapport to a highly effective level of teaching (encouraging students to think about their own experiences, having students work with each other, students complement one another in their answers, etc.). The principal misses the beginning of the lesson when the objective is stated and sees students sharing emotions about quotes and pictures that are hung throughout the room. The assignment is to write about a chosen quote or picture and then the group gets in a circle and allows volunteers to share their writing. In this scenario, I propose the following strategies for a reflective conference with the teacher:

1. Begin by talking about the components of teaching that were strong, such as respect and rapport building.

2. Be prepared to ask a question such as, "Since I was just doing a brief walkthrough, I think I missed the stated objective. Can you tell me about that?"

3. Allow the teacher to share the learning outcomes and where the lesson went after the administrator left the room.

4. Ask any lingering questions the administrator has about the direction of the lesson and the learning expected from the students.

5. Evaluate this method of conferencing versus telling a teacher "That lesson sucked."

6. Relationship building allows the teacher to feel "a part of" the process versus feeling "apart from" the process.

CHAPTER FIVE

Builder 2

Teach the Process

> *I like to encourage people to realize that any action is a good action if it's proactive and there is positive intent behind it.*
>
> —Michael J. Fox

If communication builds trust, we simply must be vigilant as administrators in making sure teachers know what we know. When trained in the new Charlotte Danielson Framework for Teaching model our county adopted in Florida, we turnkeyed that training as quickly as possible to the teachers in the district. What we knew, they knew. What they questioned, we sought to find answers. It simply wouldn't be fair, if we truly are looking at evaluations as ways to improve already good teaching, to withhold information. That would make the evaluation process seem much more like a "Gotcha!": something we were swearing to teachers it was not. I have heard administrators remark, "I'm not trying to be sneaky and withhold information from the teachers in my school, but if I tell them little bits, it will only stir up talk." Trust me on this one—the talk is going to be stirred up, with or without your solid information, however small it may seem. The problem is, without good solid information from a good, strong communicator, the talk will wind up far removed from any positive truth. Negative spins tend to have a heartier lifespan, and we can't afford that in any school or district right now. Instead, we need to remain vigilant about being proactive in our communication with faculty and staff at all times.

Many principals are feeling overwhelmed with all of the new initiatives and new tasks required by an administrator. While I am extremely sympathetic, the task still remains ever present and right in front of us. When I asked one group of teachers and administrators what pre-observation conferences had looked like in the past, several teachers could barely stifle a laugh. "What does something that doesn't exist look like?" one brave soul answered. "Hmmm . . . ," I thought. "Well, now that you have adopted this new evaluation process, it will be quite different," I ventured. One administrator raised his hand and said, "I know that we should do those pre-observation conferences, but we just don't have time. I can do the observations and spend time in the post-observation conferences, but something has to go, and I'm thinking it will be the pre-conferences." WHAT??! I shrieked. No, I didn't shriek. But I sure wanted to. How in the world are teachers and administrators going to communicate about effective planning and preparation for lessons if we don't make *time* to communicate? When the administrator made that comment, no less than ten teachers looked at me as if to say, "See? This is what we are dealing with." And no amount of "I don't have time" is going to fly with teachers. After all, if we are expecting teachers to make the time to communicate with parents, communicate with students in order to establish respect and relationships in their classrooms, and communicate effectively with other teachers in the building in order to hone their own craft, then how are we, as administrators, going to get away with saying we don't have time to communicate with the teachers who are the very essence of the school? And furthermore, why would we? "It all sounds like a really good idea in theory," the administrator continued, "but it just isn't reality." One teacher lifted her hand and timidly, but in a voice that was heard by everyone in the lecture hall, said, "But isn't that what the principals in your district did, Dr. Arneson?" "Yes," I answered, "and it took some doing to make the time to do it, but all things worth doing will get done."

Whatever we are going to inspect, we need to expect. As a new principal in 2004, I wanted to get to know more about the thinking that teachers in my school used when planning. I asked to see their lesson plans each week, with the promise that I would

1. Ask them a question or two about their thinking (written directly on their lesson plan). I explained that this may seem a bit rhetorical to them, at times, as I didn't particularly need a written or oral answer. The point, I explained, was to make them think about their own thinking (good old metacognition at work).

2. Return their lesson plans with my comments and/or questions within 24 hours.

One of the teachers who was new to our school came in my office to thank me for the explanation. At her last school, she said the principal demanded to see lesson plans but never explained the reason or the expectation. Week after week, she would get "graded" on her lesson plans without knowing the criteria for assessment. Explaining the expectation is crucial in the classroom as well as to the people teaching the classes.

In many instances across the country, school districts are rolling out new evaluation systems at the same time they are being asked to use them. "Like learning how to fly an airplane while the plane is in flight," the saying goes. Necessity breeds haste, and haste often is accompanied by misconceptions and frustration. Never would we advocate good teaching to include a frenetic sense of urgency of asking students to use a new concept without having had a chance to be taught the concept first. But that is precisely what is happening in many school districts, because of the time crunch of state and federal mandates. When district personnel or school administrators tell teachers they will be using a new evaluation system, the reason is often something akin to "Well, we've been told we have to do this, so here goes," resulting in a breeding ground for resentment.

Therefore, when the time came to adopt a new evaluation system in our county, I was pleased to see our district was proactive. We adopted the Danielson Framework for Teaching well before it would be required to do so. This gave administrators and teachers alike time for

1. Learning the process

2. Working out the kinks

3. Addressing concerns in a "pilot" fashion before the real deal

And so we began. In the true sense of putting things first things first, as Stephen Covey suggested, our district staff, all school administrators, and representatives from the teachers' union were trained on the new framework. We were not unlike many districts who truly had to make a paradigm shift in their thinking about teacher evaluations. Gone were the days of a two-ply evaluation system that basically had rated teachers either "Meets expectations" or "Unsatisfactory," a system in which approximately 95% teachers fell into the "Meets" category. On the contrary, this new system based on four distinct levels of performance described teaching, not teachers, within a lesson or block of time in which the teaching was observed. As we administrators were trained, most all of us nodded our heads like bobbing dogs hanging from the rear view mirror of the car, thinking to ourselves (and saying out loud), "Finally, a chance for teachers to demonstrate good teaching strategies in a fair and objective way." No more "Mrs. D has always done a great job. I will go in and watch her lesson but I've already filled out her evaluation for the year and she 'meets expectations.'"

Several assumptions are inherent in this shift in observing teaching:

1. *The focus is on the teaching, not the teacher:* When we observe teachers, we need to focus on the learning that is taking place. For me, the shift was even inherent in where I sat when I went in the class to observe. Instead of watching the teacher, I now was focused on the teaching and the learning. I was taking notes of specific evidence of what the teachers and students were saying and doing, not about the teacher herself or himself. For example, instead of saying, "The teacher never calls on boys. She seems to like teaching girls better than boys," I kept my notes opinion-free and instead would write, "The class is made up of 18 boys and 10 girls. Out of 22 questions asked during the whole group discussion, 20 were directed to girls." Now, we have some data about which we can discuss.

2. *Bias must be left at the door:* I cannot assume that Mrs. D is going to do a bang-up lesson, just because she has in the past. Just as important, I have to evaluate the teaching, not the mess on Ms. P's desk. I am proven wrong time after time if I assume that "messy-desk-teacher" cannot adequately teach a thorough lesson.

3. *Objectivity must reign:* I am watching for what I see and hear the teachers and students saying and doing.

4. *This is a major paradigm shift:* Teachers need time to digest this, just like I did. A fellow principal and I got together shortly after we were trained and said, "If we want to maximize the success of this new process, we simply have to put 100% effort into the training we do." Therefore, we decided to pool our knowledge and resources and train the teachers in both our schools in a team-teaching fashion. While she and I are both skilled administrators, we also recognized that we each have distinct presentation skillsets that could complement one another.

We planned for weeks before the teachers came back to school and used the first two days of "preplanning" to do an overview of the evaluation system. Our superintendent and union president had put together a video for everyone to watch that would address the obvious "first questions" everyone would have (another of Stephen Covey's seven habits: Be proactive). This is in no coincidence one of the elements of the Danielson Framework for Teaching. Component 3a talks about "communicating with students" and includes the notion that teachers should identify and address possible misconceptions. That is precisely what I feel our administration did. As Florida Senate President Don Gaetz taught me years ago when he was our district superintendent, "Don't wait for the firestorm. Get it out there. Get it all out there. Get it out there now." What an effective strategy when dealing with what, in many districts across the country, was considered a contentious issue.

We began our own Danielson training with asking teachers to identify key aspects of good teaching and then compare them to the framework. The goal was to see that, while complex, good teaching is neither mystical nor unattainable. In most cases, teachers are able to see that what is in the framework and expected on the new evaluation system is what teachers themselves agree is the hallmark of good teaching.

Since this is a book about trust and communication, I am going to be completely honest with you. The training we did, while incredibly helpful (as evidenced by the written feedback we received), was not without tension and frustration, on both the part of the teachers and on us as well. Despite recognizing that the framework is, at its very core, about good teaching, the very mention of the new evaluation system (based in part on observations but also on measures of student achievement) reduced some teachers to raw frustration and even tears.

In an effort to balance sympathy with expediting the process, we utilized several training techniques:

1. Allow a bit of "venting" at table groups.

2. Keep a "parking lot" chart for questions district administrators would need to address in the future.

3. Stick to the agenda, because, frankly, while many wanted to vent just a bit, most teachers truly want to learn about the process and not be burdened with the negativity that can result with "group think." I have a colleague who was training in a large district when frustration seemed to "win out." She continued to acknowledge the concerns for a little while but soon realized she was never going to finish teaching her agenda if she didn't change her tact. She stopped and acknowledged there was frustration continually being expressed by two or three folks (in a group of 80–90 teachers). She then asked, "By a show of hands, how many would like me to continue to address the comments?" Four hands raised. "By a show of hands, how many would like me to continue teaching about the framework?" All but four hands raised. The tribe had spoken.

4. Follow up with concerns. Don't forget those parking lots, and get people the answers to the questions they have that involve policies and procedures. Teachers, as we all do, want their concerns to be validated.

After our initial workshops, we were lucky to be given an early release day once a month, during which time we continued to teach about the specifics of the framework throughout the school year, in real time.

In the meantime, I also implemented some techniques in my own school, which many teachers indicated they appreciated.

1. In my weekly newsletter to the staff, I continued to teach about the framework, using the text of Charlotte Danielson's book (2007) to continue the learning.

2. I cited examples of particular components of the framework that I was seeing throughout our school. "Ask Angelle how she is teaching her second graders how to ask each other what they think when engaged in discussions in the classroom."

3. In faculty meetings, I would identify my own areas for growth (i.e., "That was an ineffective example of communicating with you, as I see questioning looks on many of your faces. Let me clarify." Or, I might say, "I am going to demonstrate flexibility and responsiveness [3e] to your learning needs and stop for there today so we can take a few minutes to discuss this before everyone has to leave.").

4. I began searching for books that would help teachers with specific growth areas. For example, while we know that engaging students in the lesson is the ultimate goal of teaching and learning, engaging *all* students can give even the best teachers pause. I scoured the Internet for resources to assist teachers, finding such a gem as *Total Participation Techniques* by Himmele and Himmele (2011). We ended up having a school-to-school book study using this book, one of the favorites of the teachers with whom I worked.

At the end of the first semester of implementation of the framework and our new evaluation system, I heard the following comments around our elementary school:

"This is so different than any observation I have ever had."

"The focus on what students are learning makes me realize I can't just put a good lesson on paper. I have to follow through with the implementation."

"This is the biggest learning curve I have ever experienced in my teaching career."

I also had teachers tell me that they appreciated how much time I was taking to teach them and work with them. During their beginning of the year conferences, teachers had formerly written goals for themselves that were esoteric and a bit mundane. In some cases, some teachers had even written annual goals that were exactly the same as their grade-level mates. Working on a growth model now meant we were able to see, in tandem, the specific areas in which each teacher needed some assistance, but also exactly which teachers could be a source of assistance for one another.

All of this good news about growth and collaboration hinged on one extremely important precursor: trust. I and the other administrators in my district had to believe that teachers knew that they were not the only ones for whom this new evaluation system was new. We were all learning together. At the same time, teachers had to believe that we were not going to use the new system against them. If we were going to ask teachers to bare their souls, we had to respect them enough to instill trust. As I sit and write this paragraph, I realize I should probably be using some magenta highlighting to accent these words, as this is most definitely a "make-it-or-break-it" piece to the new evaluation puzzle.

It just so happened that I was entering the dissertation phase of my doctoral program at the exact same time we were implementing the new evaluation system. It also just so happened that I had a huge interest in the builders and barriers to teacher trust in principals. And, it also just so happened that a couple of principals were none too happy with me about the timeliness of my research. "I just worry about you asking teachers if they trust us (administrators) during the time we are doing this new evaluation system," one actually said to me.

"What?" I screamed (no, I didn't scream out loud, only in my head). Isn't this the very time we *should* be determining if teachers trust us or not? And don't we need to know if they don't, so we can do something about it?

If we truly believe knowledge is power, then we simply must trust that asking for feedback and data from the people whom we serve (and I don't use the word "serve" lightly) will yield information that will help us make better, informed decisions in the future. If teachers say they are more apt to trust a principal who listens to them without asserting his or her own agenda, then we might want to consider doing the following: Listen fully while a teacher explains his or her thinking without generating our own response while the teacher is speaking. This happens to be one of my areas for growth, by the way. I sometimes find myself trying to be so intuitive, I think I know where the teacher is going with their comments or concerns before he or she is fully finished. I witnessed this happen to my colleague while we cotrained together a few months ago. During a break in our training, he was fielding a question from one of the participants. As the teacher began asking her question, my colleague began nodding his head. "What?" the teacher stopped to ask, "What do you think I'm going to say next?" All I could think was, "That could so be me." Instead of thinking we already know what is coming, we need to be willing to fully listen in order to establish and maintain a sense of trust with teachers.

Being forthcoming with information about the process and addressing concerns about observations, evaluations, and teacher pay have proved beneficial to many school districts across the country. One assistant superintendent in an upstate New York district shared with me how helpful it had been for her district administrators to get trained, training district trainers, then wasting no time at all getting every teacher in the district trained as well.

CHAPTER SIX

Builder 3

Communicate Objectively

> Dispassionate objectivity is itself a passion, for the real
> and for the truth.

> —Abraham Maslow

In researching trust, one might assume the number one contributing factor toward a high level of trust between teachers and principals would be honesty. After all, if teachers in my school are going to trust me and my judgment, doesn't that almost automatically assume a good degree of honesty exists on my part as an administrator? In reality, out of the 537 teachers who responded to one survey (Arneson, 2012) I conducted, the highest percentage of teachers indicated "communication" was the factor most contributing toward trust in their administrator.

One of the questions we must ask ourselves is whether trust builds communication or whether communication builds trust? I think it is a "chicken-egg" scenario. Just like in the song "Love and marriage . . . they go together like a horse and carriage," trust and communication are intricately intertwined. What does the end of the chorus say? "You can't have one without the other." If a teacher does not trust her principal, their communication is more likely to be tension filled. Likewise, if the communication between teacher and principal breaks down because of misunderstandings, trust will be more difficult to gain.

Trust and communication in schools are critical elements between teachers, as well. In one of the schools in which I worked, several members of a grade level came to me, separately, including the grade-level chair, to ask for help. It seems that one of their teammates became defensive and combative every time they met. The conversations looked something like this:

Beth: So, are we all set for the field trip Friday?

Jody: Yep, I was so excited I got the last of my permission slips back today.

Caren: Wait, what do you mean? Permission slips?

Joe: Yeah, I got most of mine back but am still missing two.

Caren: Wait, what do you mean? We haven't gotten permission slips yet.

Beth: Yes, remember I gave them to you on Monday.

Caren: Maybe, but you never said to send them home.

Jody: Remember? Beth sent us an email reminder. Hey it's no big deal. Send them home today.

Caren: I'll never get them back in time. See, this always happens to me.

Joe: No big deal, Caren, if you don't get them all back tomorrow, I can help you call during our planning period.

Caren: (folds arms) Never mind. I'll do it all myself. I just wish someone would have told me.

In the above example, is the problem one of communication or one of trust? Where do you see the group breaking down, and who is responsible for bringing everyone back together? Certainly, most folks will say, "Caren is acting immaturely. She needs to work together with her team better." True, and no one will argue that point. However, at the end of the day, if Caren is defensive and difficult to work with, it is likely the role of the grade-level chairperson to stand tall. That may involve everyone simply letting Caren vent without acknowledging it. It may involve saying something like, "How about if everyone sends me a return email letting me know you received my directions on how to proceed next time, just so we can make sure everyone is on the same page." One thing likely should not happen. If this is par for the course for Caren's behavior, the grade level is probably wise not to feed the beast by continually asking, "Are you okay, Caren?" Todd Whitaker talks in depth about how people often reward the behavior of complainers by allowing it to happen and by allowing the complainer's burden to be lifted and placed on the backs of the more dedicated teachers. His book *Shifting the Monkey* (2011) is all about how to prevent this from happening. Bad behavior can often be perpetuated by enabling the offender. Certainly, if this was a one-time blow-up Caren had, the person closest to her might go check on her in a little bit and make sure she is okay. Scenarios such as these often have a "wrong" way to handle them, but also many "right" ways. One way this particular grade level handled it was to appoint some-one to make sure Caren had the right information and to see if she had any questions. Did it solve all the problems? No, and there were times when the grade-level chair would come to me express-ing frustration, at which point I would need to step in. Some of the things we have to realize include that skill of seeking first to under-stand before we ourselves are understood. In other words, if some-one blows up one time, it is likely not the fault of the group. Something else bigger is likely taking place in the blower-upper's world. Sometimes, even our best efforts at reaching a resolution are dashed when we realize the other person is in need of more help than we can provide.

E-Cubed: Effective Evaluation Example

In thinking about how to proceed with communication mishaps like the one above, it is best to work for the good of the group as a whole, while ensuring that the same issue should not arise the next time (i.e., "Maybe we can avoid this problem in the future if we . . .").

While the above example is one among teachers instead of between teacher and principal, the need for building a trust-ing relationship predicated on good communication is clear and consistent. If all teachers and administrators across the country were trained on teaching expectations and observations skills in much the same way, wouldn't you expect the outcome to be pretty much consistent? Of course, this is not always the case. While some teachers in districts are saying, "This new evaluation process is helping me grow," others are saying, "My principal is looking for ways to get me." Based on the feedback I received in my research on trust and communication, there is a wide variety of emotion that plays in to the observation and evaluation process. Many teachers were gut-level honest in saying, "I want feedback on my teaching. I just don't trust my administrator's motives." I believe the major factor influencing these different perspectives is trust. But I also discovered that teachers felt the biggest trust builder in establishing trust between teachers and principals was communication. Teachers want to hear what principals have to say about the observation and teaching skills they just watched, but they also want it done in a way that is fair, equitable, and true to the process. One teacher in my survey said, "I want to know how I did but please say it respectfully."

When I ask workshop participants what kind of feedback they want after an observation, almost 100% of them say, "Objective feedback" or "Feedback without an agenda" or "Information without judgment."

As a teacher of developmentally delayed students in Dallas many years ago, I was well aware that I knew a bit more about my special needs students than my principal did. She was so sweet after observing me, and she'd say, "I couldn't do what you do. I just love watching you work with those children." To be honest, that was pretty much my reflection conference. I actually began to believe that I would need to work for a principal who had special education experience in order to get feedback on my teaching practices. But in my second year in that teaching environment, in an effort to help facilitate the inclusion of my developmentally delayed students into general education classes, I was asked to teach the rest of the teachers and the administrators some strategies I used with my special needs students. I shared behavior tips as well as strategies for communicating with students who were reluctant to participate in class. Lo and behold, as the "mystery" lifted from what I did, the feedback I received from my administrator became more specific. My principal would note, "The two boys answered questions from the story using their communication boards when directed by the teacher." Now we had something to talk about. I admit that a piece of me had enjoyed being talked about as "the one who could work with difficult children." But what was I really learning about how to help my students grow? With the advent of inclusion, I, along with many great teachers in that school, realized we had the skills to work with students with behavioral and developmental challenges as well. We just had to come up with a common language for specific strategies that worked and be able to freely talk about them.

Communicating objectively about teaching strategies, skills, and processes is precisely what is necessary for educators to improve their craft. The very nature of professional learning communities is to improve the engagement and student learning through a nonthreatening sharing and trial of practices. Take, for instance, the two examples of communicating feedback below.

1. "That lesson was so great. You really did a good job with the students. I love the book you used, and I want to use it too. It was really fun watching the students laugh with you when you gave your own example."

2. "Fourteen of the 15 students participated in the whole-group discussion about the text. The teacher asked students to think-pair-share about the question on the board. Fifteen out of 15 students accurately answered the exit card question."

While Example 1 might make a teacher feel good about his or her practice momentarily, which example has actual data to support the effectiveness of the lesson?

While working toward my counseling degree, I recall one class in which one of the interns said, "I feel like when I tell my client she is doing a good job with decision making, it will encourage her to continue to do it." The professor looked at her and asked, "But what will help your client most in continuing to make decisions that are best for her? For her to be reflective on her own decision making. Who really cares if you feel she is doing a good job or not?" While it seemed a bit harsh at the time, I get that now. For me to tell a teacher

"I loved the way you reviewed the math concept with the students" is not nearly as important as whether or not the students were able to show mastery of said math concept.

So, what are the rules of engagement for remaining objective in an observation/evaluation? My suggestions are the following:

1. MAKE IT ABOUT THE
TEACHING AND NOT THE TEACHER

When I first became a principal and did observations, I made certain I had a good seat in the classroom. What I thought that meant was sitting somewhere where I could face the teacher. I have changed my tune and now sit to the side so I can see the teacher and the learners and am able to get up and look at what the students are doing. For me, this also means eliminating my own biases about particular teachers. For example, if a teacher's desk is a mess, and I just happen to be a neat freak who always has to have a cleared-off desk, what bearing does this have on the teaching? In my own experience, I have been hard-pressed to make any connections between messy desks and teaching practice, despite the fact that it isn't the way I would do it. Principals need to be extremely conscious of their own biases and leave them at the door before entering to do an observation or an evaluation.

2. REFLECT ON THE LEARNING
THAT IS TAKING PLACE

I want to be sure I know exactly what the learning objective is when I watch a lesson or do a simple walkthrough. This means matching up what is stated or written as the objective with what the students are actually learning and doing.

3. BE SPECIFIC, AND ANSWER THE
QUESTION, "HOW DO YOU KNOW THAT?"

If I find myself thinking or writing something like, "Students understood the directions," I need to ask myself, "How do I know that?"

Were they all able to successfully master a skill? Then I need to say that. When I taught students with developmental delays, one of the skills on the aptitude test we used was "tying shoes." I couldn't very well say I thought a student "got it." I had to have proof. A successfully tied shoe was the proof in the pudding.

Communicating objectively not only entails what is written on an observation or evaluation. Communicating expectations to staff is another one of the areas that can either build or break trust. One of the participants in my study wrote, "My principal says he wants to see our lesson plans and then I get in trouble for doing them 'wrong.' Why can't you tell me what your expectations are so I know what you are looking for?" Todd Whitaker talks about how the first thing a principal new to a school should do is explain his or her expectations. He says that the front office secretary wants to know how you would like her to answer the phone. She does not, however, want to hear how she is doing it the wrong way later. In other words, in order to build trust, we need to be proactive and tell people our expectations. Simply coming behind the person and saying, "That's not how I want you to do it" or "Don't do it that way" will become a trust barrier that is tough to overcome.

Another area of communicating objectively is saying what you mean and meaning what you say. I remember when we first started asking teachers for lesson plans. Every principal in our county was "required" to pick up lesson plans and review them each week. I admit I really enjoyed this practice. It gave me a chance to see patterns and trends, keep in good touch with the skills being taught at each grade level, and make comments or ask questions about the strategies teachers were planning to use. Each week, I would print out a sticky note with a general note about best practices and maybe a quote. I would then add individual questions and comments for each teacher. I called it "my weekend homework." The problem with this practice? While every principal was required to collect lesson plans, not every principal did something with them. Some teachers reported that their principal simply threw theirs away. Some said they never received any feedback. In other words, principals were not putting any meat behind the practice. Other teachers said they would get red marks with "See me about this." They felt they were being graded but were not told to what standard they were being evaluated. Doesn't this sound like the antithesis of what we would expect our teachers to do in the classroom?

E-Cubed: Effective Evaluation Example

One example of a general sticky note that
might be adhered to lesson plans is the following:

How are you ensuring that your students show leadership
in your classroom? When you believe every student can be a
leader, our students will very often rise to the occasion of
leadership. How can you give roles and responsibilities to students?

"A new position of responsibility will usually show a
man to be a far stronger creature than was supposed."

—William James

Communication about expectations is crucial if we are going to build a community of learners. After adopting the Danielson Framework for Teaching in our district, one of the teachers in my school said one day, "I'm thinking it would make a lot of sense for me to model my lesson plan template after the components in Domain 1." Domain 1 is all about Planning and Preparation and includes Knowledge of Content and Pedagogy, Knowledge of Students, Instructional Outcomes, Knowledge of Materials/Resources, Designing Coherent Instruction, and Designing Assessments (Danielson, 2007). I honestly couldn't think of anything else that she would need to add to her lesson plan for her own planning purposes or for anyone else to understand what she would be teaching.

Consider the difference, though, between her saying that to me and me standing in front of all my faculty and telling them, "You must model your plans after this structure." I actually asked her to tell the rest of the teachers her idea and provide them a copy of the simple template she had developed using Domain 1 components as the template headings and many began using it as well.

Communicating objectively to teachers carries the expectation of effective teaching practice without all the subjective minutiae that get in the way of a teacher hearing the message of the administrator.

CHAPTER SEVEN

Builder 4

It's Not What You Say; It's How You Say It

The single biggest problem with communication is the illusion that it has taken place.

—George Bernard Shaw

A substitute teacher once told me that you could tell a lot about the culture of a school by listening to the way staff talked to one another. She said, "I sub in a lot of schools and let me tell you that you can hear it right away." She went on to say that, as a substitute teacher, she had a choice of where she wanted to work, and she was much less likely to go back to a school in which communication was a problem. I liken this to the friend of mine who said, "There are lots of great Mexican food restaurants in Tucson, Arizona. No shortage at all. I have a choice, and I am not going back to the one in which the staff couldn't communicate clearly with me OR each other."

Let me start by saying I have a pretty good idea of how we build up walls. I watched it happen, recently, when I was training in a school district. This was my second visit to the district to train administrators, and I had yet to meet the superintendent. Three hours into our second full day of training, the superintendent burst into the room, hand on one hip, and pointed an accusing finger at every administrator in the room, in turn. The administrators proceeded to be admonished for something I am not quite sure they even understood, but loosely having something to do with a training they were supposed to attend the next day.

Two minutes into what can only be described as a rant, the superintendent looked up at me, the patiently-waiting-to-finish-the-training-you-are-paying-me-to-do-trainer, and said, "Sorry for interrupting, Instructor, but I had to get that out there." I remained nameless aside from being called "Instructor." That's fine, but the bigger issue, I realized after the leader of the district slammed the door on the way out of the training room, was the fact that the administrators in the room were NOT stunned. "This happens all the time," one principal said. "Oh no, that cannot be," I thought, as I picked my jaw up off the floor "because this is the person who *runs the school district!*"

Now, I am not suggesting that just because we work in a school or school district, we are above thinking and feeling some pretty strong emotions. However, all of my experience suggests that we look like less than change for a nickel when we express our frustrations in such a way that we would never tolerate our own teachers doing in front of their students. The fact that these administrators were used to that display of raving lunacy says that this might actually be a pattern of behavior that is common to the school culture. I would suggest that it might also be a pattern of behavior on which the superintendent might consider changing.

And what kind of culture is cultivated, districtwide or schoolwide, by this type of erratic, crazed behavior?

If schools are going to run more like families than factories, as John Dewey once suggested they should, we are going to have to take a long, hard look at how we treat each other and how we talk to one another. Words are a good bit like toothpaste in a toothpaste tube. They are all in there, waiting to spring forth. However, once out in the open air, headed for the toothbrush (or, often as not, plopping down to the sink or the counter, missing its mark entirely), there is little or no chance of getting them back in the tube. Sometimes, we sure wish we could take back our words. And certainly we can apologize, which I liken to wiping up the mess of the spilt toothpaste off the counter. But the words won't ever go back in the tube or be retracted, once they are out there.

So many issues of communication skills are inherently lacking from the above example, including "being present," "be the calm in the storm instead of being the one feeding the storm," and "communicating clearly." Let's take a look at each one, in turn.

1. IN ORDER TO COMMUNICATE EFFECTIVELY, WE MUST BE PRESENT

During my first year as principal at an elementary school, we had Melissa Forney, one of my favorite writing instructors, come to our school to deliver phenomenal professional development on improving student writing in the school. When we broke for lunch, Melissa made a point of thanking me for remaining with the teachers for the training. "I totally understand you probably have other things calling for your attention, but I have always believed that teachers will follow up better with a training in which the principal attends." It doesn't quite sound like a tough call to order, does it? However, she went on to share with me that the practice of administrators remaining in professional development workshops for teachers was not the norm, but rather the exception to the rule.

What struck me most was the question of how in the world we, as school leaders, can be role models for instruction if we are not aware of the instructional practices teachers are currently exhibiting or, worse yet, being taught? Long gone are the days in which principals can sit behind the behemoth of a wooden desk while teachers are out in the trenches, learning new practices, practicing those new skills, and reflecting on the same. *School leaders need to be with teachers, learning, practicing, and reflecting together.* We need to use the training we are simultaneously receiving as fodder for our next faculty meeting, our next professional development follow-up, and even our next weekly newsletter.

E-Cubed: Effective Evaluation Example

Try this out: Add a note in the next weekly newsletter
(I called mine "Friday Focus") about a current training topic.
For example, "The first grade level to share with me how you
are incorporating a new engagement technique from our
bookstudy will win Starbuck's certificates." Trust me, staff
members will love the challenge!

In short, we need to be present, physically and mentally, in order to keep current with what is going on in the classroom. A teacher shared with me, recently, "I don't have a problem with being evaluated on a new system that ranks me and rates me and pays me for my performance on teaching competency. I have a problem with the fact that the person doing my evaluation hasn't been in my classroom one time all year." Sad to say, this conversation took place in late February, after more than half of the school year had gone by. The frustrations administrators feel when the district office staff members (or even folks from the state department of education) never darken the doorstep of their school but then make decisions that directly affect school operations are the same frustrations felt by teachers who don't feel they have a principal who is present.

In my last year as principal, we were tasked to give out 360-degree surveys to all of our teachers. The nature of a 360-degree survey is to give a full perspective of leadership from all angles (stakeholders, self, supervisor, etc.). "What a great way to thoroughly and anonymously find out how we are doing as administrators," I thought. Once we gave out the surveys, we found out that, not only would the survey be filled out by teachers, but a designated supervisor would also fill it out on our work. Much to my surprise, the supervisor who filled out my 360-degree survey had not been in our school one time that entire school year. She even told me, "I don't get any parent complaints from your school at all, so I know you're doing a good job." While the input from the teachers was well-rounded and thoughtful, it was hard to put much stock in the ratings from my supervisor when she didn't see what I was doing. Everyone feels this way, including teachers who wonder how a principal who never sets foot in their classroom could adequately, let alone fairly, evaluate their performance.

Administrators need to take the time to hear the issues weighing on the hearts and minds of teachers, and that means we can't hide behind a closed door all day. Several respondents in the research on trust (Arneson, 2012) have mentioned that behavior, specifically: "He never comes out of his office"; "She hides behind her closed door"; "I know she is busy but come out of there—we need a principal around here!"; and many others.

But how can everyone get involved in creating a culture of being present? Just like the cartoon on the following page (Jantoo) depicts teachers not always being ready to face another day at school, principals often feel the same way.

Figure 7.1

"I know the kids don't like you and pick on you, but you have to go to school...you're the teacher."

Source: Cartoon Stock. Used with permission.

Teachers and school leaders share more than we sometimes admit. The school leader is the head of the school, and the teacher is the head of his or her classroom. Principals and teachers, alike, need to know what is going on in all aspects of their work domain. What does this mean? For teachers, it means there should never be any areas of the classroom they cannot reach. Even if they teach in a crowded classroom crammed full of desks, letting any area become a place that can't be reached by walking your beat is dangerous. What happens when teachers let an area of their class go unmonitored or unchecked? We know exactly what happens in that spot—whispering, note passing, and sometimes much worse. No, every area of the classroom must be accessible to the teacher, if for no other reason than accountability and presence.

In much the same way, *principals need to strive to be present in all parts of the school for at least some time each day.* I had a principal tell me once that he never returned to his office from lunch the same way. I thought it was an interesting concept, as it reminded me of all the workout gurus who say to vary your routine in order to stay in shape. In a way, this is achieving that goal. We'll stay more "leadership fit" if we are present and know what is going on in all aspects of the school. If you ask principals and teachers whether they eat lunch in the staff lounge, you are likely to get a plethora of responses. Some people feel the need to take a break from all the school chatter and just sit quietly in their rooms or offices with the lights turned off, listening to music playing softly in the background. Other staff members realize lunchtime may be the only time they are truly able to get a bit of adult conversation and choose, therefore, to visit the lounge for this reason. As a principal, I always felt as though eating lunch in the lounge on occasion was a great way to connect with the teachers and staff. However, I also found it terribly difficult to break away from the office or the lunchroom during lunchtime, so I understand both points of view.

But what do we do about those times in which we are confronted with folks who could earn frequent flyer miles getting our attention? Teachers certainly know the feeling—the student who, as soon as you walk by his desk, has a question for you. School leaders also know the feeling—the teacher who hears you walk by his classroom and has to pull you in to show you something or ask you something. At times like these, we may even feel frustrated and wish we could run away.

Instead of dismissing them, which never seems to solve the problem, there might be a better solution. Simply *give them the time with a limit.* So, it might look like this: When the frequent flyer gets your attention ("for the 100th time today," you are thinking but not saying), begin by saying, "I know you have students to attend to, so if you have something quick I can answer . . ."

E-Cubed: Effective Evaluation Example

Try this out: When someone seems to monopolize your attention, try setting limits instead of putting them off. Remember, it's not what you say; it's how you say it. We need to role-model for others how we want to be treated. Imagine if you were someone else's "needy" person.

Some days, it would be nice to simply run and hide, but the problem is the issues from which we are running and hiding are still there when we do finally pick ourselves up and face them. That is why I love that story about "Eating the Frog." The story suggests that if we woke up every morning and ate a frog the first thing, the day would likely get better from there. In other words, eating the frog is probably the worst the day can bring to you. So, why not eat the frog first? I shared this with my faculty during preplanning one year and asked, "What is your 'frog'?" The answers mainly consisted of the following: calling parents back, taking care of paperwork that must get done, and facing a parent at the door of your classroom whom you know is angry. Remarkably, my list was fairly similar, but it sometimes also included "calling in a teacher to discuss a sensitive issue that needs to be addressed." Take, for example, the time when a parent has called and accused the classroom teacher of being flexible on several students' grades but not at all flexible on the grades of this parent's child. What is your initial reaction? Some people say, "I'm not even going to address it. The teacher and parent will work it out." Others will say, "How dare that teacher do that to this student? I'm giving her a reprimand this afternoon." Neither reaction factors in talking to the teacher first before deciding his or her fate.

In the end, we want to find the right balance for handling situations like this, while we are trying to effectively lead the school. The point is, we need to be present in our effort to make something happen and not feel as if we have gone overboard in our reaction. Finding the right balance means not going too far to either end of the Reaction Continuum (see Figure 7.2).

After talking about our frogs, we all agreed, however, that whatever our frog was, it didn't taste any better letting it wait until later in the day. In fact, it actually was more satisfying (if you're squeamish,

Figure 7.2   Reaction Continuum

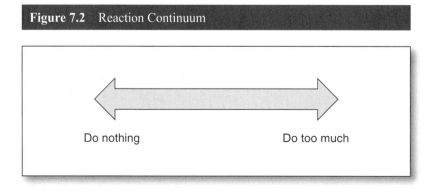

Do nothing   Do too much

you might want to remove the frog analogy at this point) to get it over with. Why is this? The angry parent gets their concern addressed sooner than later, thereby validating that we truly do care. Likewise, the teacher knows where he or she stands with the principal and is given a chance to explain and to work things out with the student and the parent.

Therefore, being present means making ourselves available, approachable, and vigilant in the search for better communication with the teachers with whom we work.

2. BE THE CALM IN THE STORM INSTEAD OF BEING THE ONE FEEDING THE STORM

I worked with a principal who knew exactly how to send her staff into a frenzy. She'd come back from a particularly contentious district meeting, one in which we heard of some new and devastating change to the current way we were doing things (what might it say about the way we worry and blow things out of proportion when I can't quite remember what one of those devastating issues was, in the first place?). She'd gather all her teachers in a meeting, saying "Whatever you were planning to do this afternoon, please cancel. I have to talk to you immediately!" Once all were gathered, she would tell them the news in an excited tone of voice, getting them all riled up with "Oh no! How can they do that to us?" I had visions of kids spinning each other around on the merry-go-round, enjoying the way the kids on the platform would start to scream and try to hold on for dear life as the merry-go-round spun faster and faster, out of control. It may seem like fun being the spinner until everyone that is out of control on the merry-go-round starts getting sick or falling off the equipment.

Some teachers have a knack for doing this, as well. Before the high-stakes test, teachers who tell horror stories of how many students failed last year are guilty of the same. Quit spinning people out of control! I, personally, think our job as educators and school leaders is tough enough to keep all the people *from* freaking out. Why in the world would you want crazed people on your hands?

Instead, why not be the calm in the storm?

Even if we are feeling a bit frenetic about a new initiative or expectation or requirement we are expected to uphold, why not come to the collective table with an attitude of solution orientation? Setting the expectation for success is not that foreign, is it? In fact, it sounds vaguely familiar to what we expect all teachers to foster with their own students. Every teacher knows that he or she has the power to shake students up with a sentence, "Standardized testing starts tomorrow and we never even got to the chapter on multiplying fractions!!" But instead, the savvy educator, setting that expectation for excellence, says, "I was so pleased with the progress you made on the last assessment. You guys are going to ROCK this standardized test tomorrow, and I am going to be here to witness the whole thing!"

E-Cubed: Effective Evaluation Example

How can you turn this statement around to show you are the calm in the storm?

"I know everyone is freaking out about the new evaluation system. Trust me, I am too."

The important part is to acknowledge their trepidation but believe in and convey that belief in their success.

How do we foster this calm atmosphere in a schoolwide environment? Here are my top five strategies:

1. *Communicate to stakeholders (students, parents, teachers, and staff) all pertinent information* (i.e., "We will now be having a lockdown drill. Everyone move quickly to your places.").

2. *Focus on the positive* when possible (i.e., "We had some areas in which we need to improve before the next drill, but overall I am proud of the work you did.").

3. *Use a calm tone of voice.* Let's face it. A calm and even tone of voice always sounds more assuring than a frenetic, high-pitched worry-filled voice.

4. *Give feedback in a timely fashion.* In the case of a drill, sending home a note with students letting parents know what happened that day will save you TONS of phone calls the next day.

5. *Remember, you are the leader of the group.* People are relying on the leader of the school to set the tone. In the 1989 movie

Immediate Family, Glenn Close's character explains the need, in marriage, for no more than one person to be allowed to be crazy at any one time. The point is—someone always needs to be the sane one.

3. COMMUNICATE CLEARLY

My father called a few weeks ago to tell me he was trying to collect on a $4000 life insurance policy for my mother, whom he divorced 30 years ago and who died 7 years ago. He needed me to provide the company with details of her death in order to collect. When I called the insurance company and gave them my mother's death certificate information, the lady said, "We'll send you the $1000 right away." "Oh," I said with a bit of surprise, "my dad thought the policy paid out $4000." (Anyone see where this is going?) She almost chuckled and said, "I told your dad it was for a thousand dollars, not four thousand dollars." Misunderstanding? For sure. Wishful thinking? Perhaps. What could have cleared this up, sooner than later? A good dose of paraphrasing or repeating back what you think you heard.

Communication, according to the University of Colorado's Conflict Resource Consortium (CRC), has a sender and a receiver. The sender has information he or she intends to express to the receiver, who must interpret the information. Clarity of word choice can easily affect the message. Expression of a message, either spoken or written, is a key aspect of successful communication. Teachers surveyed in Arneson's research (2012) indicated they appreciated a principal who spoke clearly, articulated what he or she thought, and had a pleasing tone of voice.

Communicating clearly equates, in part, to communicating effectively. You can't have one without the other. It's that love and marriage thing again. They go together like a horse and carriage. Tone of voice can make the difference between taking a statement to heart and taking offense to the same statement.

E-Cubed: Effective Evaluation Example

Say the following statement, using different tones of voice. How does the message change?

"I noticed you were on the phone when you picked up your students from lunch today."

Tone of voice can make all the difference in the world in the above statement. Did anyone say it in a concerned tone, as if to say, "I was worried about you. Is everything okay?" Most of us read that and jump to the conclusion that someone just got scolded, and that certainly could be the case. We need to make sure our tone of voice matches the sentiment we mean to convey.

Ambiguous messages can lead to interpretation, as well, which can be dangerous. When a principal says to his staff, "I need to see your lesson plans soon," what does that mean? For some, "soon" may mean by this afternoon; others may interpret that as later this week. We need to be as clear as possible in order to avoid ambiguity and the resulting misinterpretation. If a teacher comes to see me and says, "I'd like to speak with you when you can," telling him we can meet "soon" will surely not be enough. Never has the need to be specific meant so much to me as when my husband and I moved to Arizona, a state in which there is no observance of time change. Thus, when someone from the east coast says, "Let's have a teleconference at 10:00 tomorrow," I always clarify with "Do you want to meet 10:00 a.m. your time?" and then I will adjust accordingly.

Why is this so important? Maybe it's because people take miscommunication so personally. Many times, when relationships are filled with tension or they fail entirely, it is because of a miscommunication. And we tend to blame it on the other person. He said, she said is much more likely to be the cause of the problem than, "I wasn't clear when I said . . ." We often hear what we expect to hear or want to hear, which can greatly add to the difficulty. After K.C., our first Labrador retriever died, I was ready within weeks to get a new puppy. My sentimental husband, Dave, wanted to grieve K.C.'s death a bit more. When I asked, "Can we at least think about a puppy?" after seeing a litter of pups advertised in the paper, he answered, "We can think about it." I was off and running. I had heard all I needed to hear to be convinced we were both ready to go puppy hunting. He was only ready to think about when might be an acceptable grieving time. (We got Rudy, our new Labrador retriever, 2 months later.) (Arneson, 2011b, *Letting Go of K.C.*)

CREATING A CULTURE OF EFFECTIVE COMMUNICATION IN SCHOOLS

A few years ago, our elementary school decided to focus on leadership. We decided we wanted to change the way students and staff spoke to one another. So, at the beginning of the year, we had a news show with two puppets (Labrador retrievers—Libby who always did the right thing and Mud who always was confused and did the wrong thing) talk to each other. When Mud would say something not-so-nice, Libby said to her, "We don't talk like that at Edge." Lo and behold, the students started picking up on that lingo. They began telling each other "We don't talk like that at Edge" when someone would say something mean or hurtful. Some would even throw in "Libby said so" for good measure. It began sticking.

It actually became a teaching point when a new student would enter the school. Imagine a new student sitting in a classroom when the teacher is about to start the lesson on plants and seeds. The new student looks at his or her tablemates and, obviously trying to get the attention of the mates, says, "This is stupid." The other three classmates at his table quietly turn to the new student and whisper, "We don't talk like that at Edge." Pollyanna? Impossible to achieve? Not in the least. The above scenario actually happened . . . in a kindergarten classroom. Fifth graders may have said it with a different tone of voice, but the common denominator was they were all saying it. It became part of the culture and climate of our school.

E-Cubed: Effective Evaluation Example

Talk with others in your school. What do you want
the communication in your school to look like? Sound like?

Adopt a "mantra" you can use, schoolwide,
such as "We don't talk like that at _____."

CHAPTER EIGHT

Builder 5

Follow-Up With Honesty and Support

Real-time action of the leaders inspires the followers and the support-seeking word of the followers motivates the leaders.

—Anuj Somany

So, if we know what teachers feel are barriers to trust, then it should be fairly easy to identify what they do want and need. Right? The easy answer is, administrators simply need to communicate with the teachers in their school. Apparently, this is easier said than done, as many teachers feel their principals are not using effective communication. And teachers and principals need to collectively and individually make the commitment to be open and straightforward with one another at all times. Communication, however, is even more crucial in a time in which administrators play an active role in the evaluations and, increasingly, in the pay of teachers. Not surprisingly, what teachers clamor for more than being exempt from this type of accountability is someone they can trust giving them accurate and honest feedback about their teaching. And, in order to accomplish this, good communication is a must-have.

Traditionally, post-observation conferences between teachers and administrators went something like this. After the observation, the teacher was called to the office to meet with the principal. The teacher sat on the other side of the desk and the principal pulled out the observation paperwork, either a checklist, tally sheet, narrative, or some combination of the three. The principal would say, "I really liked the activity you did with the kids. They seemed to like it, too," to which the teacher would breathe a sigh of relief. Or, the principal would say something like, "You didn't give enough wait-time between questions and calling on students. Try to do that more," to which the teacher might also breathe a sigh of relief that the principal didn't notice anything more glaring. The principal would then push the paper over to the teacher's side of the desk, ask him or her to sign it, and make a copy for their records. Less than 10 minutes was likely spent on such an endeavor. In one district in New Jersey, several teachers told me they would have appreciated the above scenario. Their post-observation conference consisted of a phone call from the secretary, asking them to stop by the secretary's desk during their planning time and sign off on the evaluation. What?! How can that be? It's called a "post-observation conference," not a drive-by signing. But, again, some teachers say, "At least I didn't have to sit there in the principal's office, listening to her critique my lesson when she knew nothing about what I teach." Clearly, administrators are not communicating well if we are not able to share our knowledge of the lesson taught by our dialogue after the observation, or at the very least, admit, "I may not have known that much about music theory before I walked in your room, but your lesson plan and the preplanning conference helped make me smart enough to know what I would be watching." Don't we owe at least that professional courtesy to the teachers in our school? The answer is a resounding yes!

HONESTY

Honesty is the first chapter in the book of wisdom.

—Thomas Jefferson

The history of genocide may seem an odd topic in an educational book. But trust me. When the Turkish government decided to kill upwards of one and a half Armenians in the early 1900s, careful planning and rational experimentation were needed for optimum success. So they practiced with dogs first. Cleansing Constantinople of the thousands of dogs that roamed free provided an opportunity to test a method that could be later used on the Armenians. The dogs were taken to a desert island far enough away from the mainland that they would not be able to swim back, although many tried. The thought seemed to be, "Get them out of our way. The problem will disappear." What they didn't count on was that the winds would carry the sound of the barking dogs back to shore, if not the dogs themselves.

The analogy is the fact that the problem is still around, sometimes even more tragically, even though we aren't staring it straight in the face. As sad as it is to hear that anyone would try to get rid of thousands of dogs by just moving them and then turning away in hopes to not have to deal with them is insane. In an effort to eradicate the problem without having to face it head-on, we can cause ourselves more grief than if we simply face an issue honestly and in a forthright fashion. A great leader once taught me, "When there is an issue to address, get it out there. Get it all out there. And, whatever you do, get it out there sooner than later." Don Gaetz, who was a superintendent in Florida, went on to become the president of the Florida Senate. By telling me this sound advice, he was teaching me a great lesson about leadership when we had a potential outbreak of the SARS virus in our community. While some folks whispered, "Let's not say anything unless someone asks us about it first," Don Gaetz called for a press conference at our elementary school and addressed any and all concerns. Not every parent or community member was thrilled with the information that was given, but they seemed to respect the upfront and honest nature by which it was shared. Robert E. Lee said, "The trite saying that honesty is the best policy has met with the just criticism that honesty is not policy. The real honest man is honest from conviction of what is right, not from policy." In other words, are we simply telling the truth to say we told the truth, or are we telling the truth because the truth will help move us forward and keep us from having bigger problems down the road?

Serious misfortunes, originating in misrepresentation, frequently flow and spread before they can be dissipated by truth.

—George Washington, letter to
John Jay, May 8, 1796

Schools are breeding grounds for another deadly virus called "the rumor." We are all familiar with the phenomenon. Someone hears of a conversation about his or her school, and even though the person may not know all the details (or any, for that matter), he or she somehow feels compelled to tell someone else "I heard something about money and next year." And there the craziness ensues. "Do you think they'll lay off the art teacher?" "I don't know; I heard the school down the road may be having to get rid of a copy machine. Maybe we will, too!" "Oh no! I wonder if they are going to close our school. They are doing that in other places, you know." Pretty soon, the experiences that other schools or districts have had become our own possibilities and even probabilities. And we're off and running. Getting the information out there as quickly and efficiently as possible is clearly the best bet, as the news may not be popular, but it is the true news. No more crucial time exists for honesty and forthrightness than when a school, district, state, or nation is implementing a new type of high-stakes evaluation system.

It was no surprise that teachers in the research on trust (Arneson, 2012) indicated they had higher trust in administrators who were honest and forthcoming. Other trust builders in the honesty category included: *sharing information with all, not just a select few; keeping promises; open kimono; honest about teacher performance; honest about district happenings; honest even if it is controversial.* It is clear that students, teachers, parents, and administrators want honesty from all stakeholders. Reina and Reina (2006) said that leaders are and should be employees' best source of information. The problem occurs when staff members hear pertinent information from other sources, so the timing, accuracy, and honesty are crucial in this case.

Bryk and Schneider (2002), in *Trust in Schools,* said individuals tend to withdraw their trust when people don't meet their expectations. In other words, trusting someone is a choice we make. The choice is based on past benefits or risks experienced in the relationship (http://psychology.about.com/od/sindex/g/soci alexchange.htm) and can influence future choices and the outcome of the relationship.

Schools are no exception to the experience of trust. The relationships between staff and administration are based on past experiences as well. Administrators and teachers trust each other, or not, because of past chances for the other to be honest.

E-Cubed: Effective Evaluation Example

Think about the relationships you have
with the teachers in your school. On what past
experiences are those relationships based?
How do those experiences impact your
observations and evaluations of the teachers?

In *Smart Trust* (2012), the author Stephen M. R. Covey tells the story of the CEO of a technology company who was approached by Apple's Steve Jobs to try out their software. Jobs called Morgan, the CEO, and said he wanted to model Morgan's product at a big Macworld event but needed the code. Morgan's management team members looked at each other and shook their head no at Morgan. The company wasn't in the market to risk losing their intellectual property. Jobs told Morgan, "You're just going to have to trust me." Going against the shaking heads of his management team, Morgan gave Jobs the code. In the end, Jobs gave lots of kudos to the new technology at his Macworld event in 1998, creating great publicity for Morgan.

But what past experience did Morgan use to trust Jobs' honesty? Perhaps none, except his public reputation. Morgan simply did what he thought was best in this situation, which was to trust his instincts when it came to Jobs. Which brings up an interesting point. Perhaps, sometimes, we are somehow willing to trust from the outset of a relationship.

My own experience with researching trust bore that out as well. Teachers were asked about the degree to which they trusted their administrators, and those findings were disaggregated by length of time the teacher had worked with a principal. The results varied significantly between those who had worked for their principal for less than a year and those who had worked with their principal for more than 10 years. In workshops, I ask participants to guess the outcome. Many guess that the greater trust occurred with teachers and administrators who had worked together for more than 10 years. There definitely was a difference . . . but in the opposite direction. The average rating of trust for the teachers who have worked for the current principal for less than a year was 4.71 on a scale of 5. The average rating for the teachers who have worked for the current principal for more than 10 years was a 3.18. That is a difference of 1.5 on a small scale of 5.

When I ask teachers and principals to guess why this would be, they give answers such as, "The longer we work together, the more chances there are to mess up," "Distrustful deeds add up over time," and many others.

The genocide story is indicative of how many of us feel about this tender subject. Teachers might say, "I know some of my parents or students don't trust me, but I sure don't want to know." Principals may find themselves saying, "Oh no. Don't ask the teachers if they trust me. We just started a new evaluation system this year, and I am having to be tough on them so they might say bad things." Do district staff really want to know how much help schools feel like they give them? In other words, we can all tout honesty and forthrightness, but we need to make sure we are not allowing ourselves to bury our heads in the sand. This seems to be what happened to the dogs in 1910 in Constantinople.

Dealing with trust in an effective manner is going to require willingness, a level of willingness that not everyone will be ready to have right away. The good news is that honesty and trust are contagious. The more we show the willingness to move forward to make our school more successful, the more that willingness is perpetuated.

If we have a choice to be on a cycle of honesty and trustworthiness or the vicious cycle of dishonesty and a reputation of distrust, we need to ensure we are choosing the former and not the latter and making every attempt to live our lives each and every day as if we want to be remembered for the latter.

There is a cartoon going around social media that depicts Wile E. Coyote. The caption alongside it says, "It's sad how Wile E. Coyote is remembered for his violence, and not for his brilliant paintings of tunnels." What a simple but purposeful thought. If we are not careful about the way we act and react, we will most assuredly be remembered for the negative aspects of our personalities.

Building Honesty

In speaking to teachers and administrators across the country, I hear many say things like, "She hasn't lied to me that I know of, I just don't trust that she is being completely honest." What gives us that feeling of honesty and trustworthiness in a person? Many say it's the person's track record. Even if the individual hasn't personally lied to us, we observe things that seem a little shady. One man told me, "She has proven not to be honest one too many times." When I pushed him to tell me if his supervisor had lied to him, he admitted, "Maybe not, but I watch the way she handles things, and I see her bending the truth to meet her needs." I heard a pastor say that lies first ruin honesty, next they ruin reputations, and finally (and most drastically) they ruin relationships entirely. A good rule of thumb might be to ask ourselves before telling a falsehood, "Am I willing to gamble with honesty, my reputation, and the relationships that might be affected by this statement?"

And trust regarding honesty is certainly a schoolwide issue, not one that can be solely owned by the teachers or the administration. In *The Speed of Trust* (2006), Stephen M. R. Covey's said his father eloquently taught him, "If you think the problem is *out there,* that very thought is the problem." Doesn't that remind you of that saying, "When you are pointing the finger at someone else, just remember there are three more fingers pointing back at you"? Never has it been so crucial for schools to embrace the concepts of trust, honesty, and shared responsibility than now.

Dishonesty, therefore, does not need to take on the form of lying to and cheating on a spouse, although that is certainly a form of dishonesty. Honesty is also about reputation. For example, a friend and I tried to get together for lunch. I suggested a local Mexican restaurant. She cried out, "Uggh! Anywhere but there!" I asked why and she told me the story of calling the restaurant to get reservations for her family for her husband's birthday. The owner, herself, said, "I will pick a special table for your family, and we'll have it ready by 6:30." When the family arrived, there was no reserved table, and furthermore, there were no tables available until 8:30! The owner was nowhere to be found. My friend said, "Never again. The owner lied to me." Likely, we can all sit and armchair quarterback this one, right? "The restaurant should have a policy in which reservations are confirmed by phone or email." The problem with reputations is we sometimes don't get a second chance to make it right. Worse yet, in the case of this restaurant example, the friend would likely earn frequent flyer points or a black belt in reviewing on Trip Advisor. She wrote a scathing review of her experience on the website that will live in infamy, no matter how great I think the food is. Her point was, in a city of great Mexican restaurants, I will make another choice than to choose the one who lost my trust. Trust,

Reina and Reina (2006) say in their book *Trust and Betrayal in the Workplace,* is easy to lose and hard to regain, making it a fragile aspect of any relationship.

How does honesty in your own school fare? What is the reputation of the school? The administration? Office staff? Teachers? One way to find out is to do a climate survey. In the district in which I was a principal for 7 years (and a guidance counselor for 9 years prior to that), every parent was invited to fill out a climate survey annually. Now, the questions may not have exactly been about "Is the teacher honest?" or "Does the principal tell me the truth?" but the questions that were asked were likely answered based, in part, on our honesty. "The teacher informs me regularly of my child's progress" and "The principal is the right leader for this school" are descriptor phrases that will generate a good bit of talk among the general public if honesty is not present.

Of course, it's one thing to administer the survey, a whole other process to analyze the results. We had teachers in our school who would come back after the results went "live" and give me the best data analysis, such as, "You know, the office staff here truly is the best. I compared the opinions about our school against the other schools in our area, and our office staff rocks!" Another would analyze the data of our not-as-strong area, "The area in which we need the most improvement is helping parents understand the value in homework because that was where most of our disgruntled opinions fell." Kudos to those who are interested in analyzing data such as these. Of course, I always had to talk someone down from the ledge when the outlier parent or lone wolf (and thankfully, it was only on a very rare occasion that this occurred) would say something mean and hateful like "This is the worst school ever. Why don't you just close the doors?"

And we need to take the time to celebrate the areas in which we are doing well. The next step, of course, is establishing a plan of action in order to improve on the weak areas.

1. Develop a survey based on trust in the school and its staff. If your school or district doesn't already have one, I suggest using Survey Monkey. It's easy to develop, easy for participants to use, and can be free or very low-cost.

2. Administer the survey (we have found most folks have online access, but we always set aside a computer in the Media

Center or Computer Lab for those parents who did not and wanted to stop by and fill it out).

3. Analyze the results, taking the outliers with a grain of salt. I have a friend who consults with me. She had someone tell her on an evaluation form, once, that they didn't like her blouse. My response? "Outlier." Well, I may have called the person insane as well, but it was definitely an outlier. It also fell in the category of "So what and who cares?"

4. Take time to celebrate achievements.

5. Develop a plan of action to improve on the weaker areas.

Now the question: Do you really want to know the results? I admit my trepidation the first time I expanded the concept of our district climate survey to also administer one of my own to our staff. I felt I was really putting myself out there. And there were a couple of tough pills to swallow when I got the results (one person indicated she was nervous around me, and another teacher said I should be tougher on student discipline). However, after rolling around in my self-pity for a little while, I had to ask myself, "Didn't I really want to know in the first place? Knowing there is a problem, after all, is the first step to fixing the problem, right?" As my husband jumped to remind me, "The good overwhelmingly outweighed any little negative feedback you got," I still focused on those few negative comments. How can that be when I teach workshops on good leadership and am always looking for a positive message in each event? Hmmm . . . maybe because honesty is HARD, honestly!

When faced with results from a survey such as this (Have your teachers ever surveyed your students? Parents?), the task is to take the bulk of the responses, analyze them, and make adjustments as appropriate. If you survey 75 people, and one of them says you make snap judgments, it may be a one-time experience. However, if 10 of them say you say one thing and do another, that might actually be something worth examining. What adjustments can you make to address that issue?

In our schools, we also need to examine the level of comfort in honestly expressing our opinions? For example, do teachers feel comfortable honestly sharing their thoughts on the observation the principal just conducted without fear the principal might go back in and change a rating if the teacher disagrees? It works in all aspects of the school as well. Do principals feel comfortable sharing their feelings with faculty and staff without fear someone will run to the union representative and complain, "You won't believe what he said to me." A principal just shared with me last week that she was frustrated that every time she started to talk to one of the teachers in her school about a concern (a parent phone call, a reminder about protocol, etc.), the teacher would ask, "Do I need to call our union rep in here to meet with us?" Certainly, if we have cause to believe we are unjustly being accused of something, we should use all of our legal resources possible. However, starting every conversation with this question reeks of a bit of paranoia and possibly even a threat. This is clearly not the way to build relationships between staff.

So, how can we build honesty as a pervasive trait throughout the school? I propose the following three techniques:

1. Role model honesty and admitting mistakes.

2. Start with the least restrictive and intrusive method of sharing an honest concern.

3. Stop and listen to the other person's concern before reacting.

Let's look at them, one at a time.

1. Role model honesty and admitting mistakes.

One thing we know to be true about creating an environment of respect and rapport in the classroom is our students need to feel safe about making mistakes or they won't participate in class. Charlotte Danielson (2007) felt this classroom environment was so incredibly important that it warranted one entire domain (out of four) on her framework for teaching.

So, if a student raises his hand and the teacher demeans him in front of the rest of the class, the student will likely not raise his hand any time real soon. On the flip side, when the climate of a class is such that when a student raises her hand and is wrong and the teacher says something like, "Whew, I'm glad someone else said that. I thought that was the answer, too, until I read this part in the book." In other words, let's make it okay for students to err and still save face. Furthermore, if there is any teasing that happens by students to one another, the teacher needs to be the barometer for that. If it is teasing that turns even remotely toward bullying, it needs to be nipped right away. However, the teacher can create an environment where everyone is allowed to laugh at themselves and support one another or one in which students are caustic to one another.

2. Start with the least restrictive and intrusive method of sharing an honest concern.

As in the example of the teacher who kept asking her principal, "Do I need to call my union representative in here to meet with us?" building trust and honesty requires a bit of willingness to trust without expecting the worst. A human resources director with whom I once worked said to me, "I like to give people the benefit of the doubt." What that means to me is if a principal gets one parent phone call complaining that a teacher has called a student "Dumb," perhaps that principal doesn't need to immediately call the superintendent or human resources director to have the teacher berated publicly. Perhaps, the principal can first assess the situation with the teacher and give the teacher a chance to apologize to the student and the class, if the offense was made. I once told a child to "scoot" back to the classroom after reprimanding him for being disrespectful to his teacher. The next thing I knew, his parents called the assistant superintendent to tell him I had called their son another "s" word that ends in a "t." Apparently, "scoot" was misunderstood. How about before we sue McDonald's over being given incorrect change, we simply take a minute to allow people to make things right, in the least intrusive way possible?

After being charged too much for a chair we bought at a home furnishings store, I asked the salesperson if she could change the amount we had been charged. She said she couldn't without a manager approving it. I called back later that day, when the manager was in, and asked her to take care of it for me. When she was reluctant to do so, citing the fact that we had already bought it, I asked, "I would really appreciate it if we can get this worked out and you would refund our money. Can you make that happen?" She then changed the charge on my credit card. I didn't need to make a scene, I simply needed to state my concern, honestly and professionally.

3. Stop and listen to the other person's
concern before reacting.

Be honest. Have you ever had someone come to you with a concern and you already know how you are going to react before they are finished with their first sentence? Maybe it's because you have past history with the person before you. Maybe it's because you just had a disagreement with your spouse that morning. Maybe it's because you just aren't taking the time to listen.

Whatever the reason, when we shut people down without allowing them to finish speaking, we rob them of the chance to share their thoughts honestly and openly. My first year as a principal, I was so desirous to have a perfect school, I found myself frustrated when any parent would complain about a teacher to me. "That can't be. Mrs. Robins has never said anything like that before," I said more than one time. I had a parent who was also a friend who was honest enough with me to tell me, "When you say that to me, I feel like you don't believe what I am telling you." I'm not saying I ever was perfect after that, but I certainly tried to be cognizant of how my words had the potential to shut down the other person's train of thought or concern.

One teacher I knew always started shaking her head as soon as I would begin telling her something she felt was controversial. It's as if she was saying, "No, no, no . . . don't say anything I don't like." It certainly hindered honest communication. Another friend opens her mouth in astonishment if someone begins to share an honest concern with her. A gentleman with whom my husband used to work would say, "yeah, yeah, yeah" intermittently while another person spoke, as if to hurry them up. None of these behaviors instill the desire to open up and share more. We need to be conscious of our verbal and nonverbal behavior when another person is expressing a concern to us. Rolling eyes, interrupting, hand gestures that say "hurry up" will not encourage more honesty. Paraphrasing the concern, listening all the way through the concern, and maintaining an encouraging posture will all aide in the communication process.

As a former guidance counselor, I taught students from kindergarten through eighth grade how to make I-messages (model in Figure 8.1). The rules of I-messages are the following: Start with "I," tell how you feel without blame, tell the other person why you feel that way, and finish with how you think the issue could be resolved.

Figure 8.1 School Community Elements

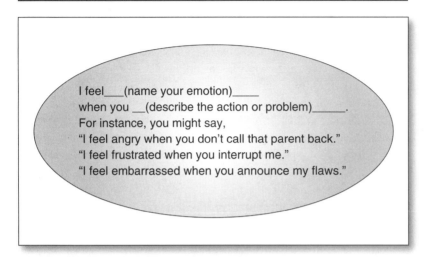

I feel___(name your emotion)___
when you __(describe the action or problem)_____.
For instance, you might say,
"I feel angry when you don't call that parent back."
"I feel frustrated when you interrupt me."
"I feel embarrassed when you announce my flaws."

What I always found fascinating was how many staff members would tell me, "I sure am glad I was in the class or the auditorium when you taught those I-messages. I needed a refresher course on those." Lo and behold, when we use them, things seem to get better. There are no guarantees, of course, but I have found a remarkable correlation between using I-messages and how well my husband and I get along.

Even grade-level mates can use I-messages in their group meetings. One grade level I know used an actual stuffed elephant (to build on the elephant in the room metaphor) in their meetings. If you had a concern you wanted to share, it was your turn to address the elephant in the room. The rule was, let's address it civilly so it doesn't get out of hand and ugly. Another grade level asked for a mediator when they felt their honest concerns might end up hurting some feelings. Having a neutral mediator (which ended up being me) was a way to minimize the emotions felt when honest statements were made.

Being honest and true to one another in a school setting also requires us to take certain precautions against gossip and ill-speaking. The confidential secretary (with whom I worked for 7 years as a principal) and I used to have the need to speak confidentially about parent concerns or other school-related issues. We learned the hard way not to have these conversations in the middle of the front office, because no matter how quiet we thought we might be talking, Murphy's Law dictated that if we were speaking about a particularly difficult parent, that parent would walk through the door. And what does that say about my integrity in hearing a confidential concern of a parent's or a teacher's if they see that I am not able to keep other people's information confidential?

Honesty simply remains one of those most vital cornerstones to trust. If I, as the principal, say I expect teachers to be honest with their students and parents, then I should certainly grant the same courtesy and respect to teachers and other staff members. If teachers say they have a no-cheating or no-lying policy in the classroom, then they should be very cautious of how they present themselves even when they think students aren't watching. Honesty makes up our reputation, and our reputations matter.

SUPPORT

When I first started teaching, I worked in a great, old, inner-city school in San Antonio. I loved my children in my class who all had labels of severely emotionally disturbed, but I honestly can't remember the names of 10 of the teachers there. The principal was sweet, but he didn't come to my classroom much. After the first couple of weeks of trying to figure out what to do with these students, who turned out to be remarkably curious and willing to learn new things once they knew I believed they could, the principal knew I could handle what went on in my classroom. I never sent children to the office. The other teachers kept a safe distance from my children, as well, and maybe from me, too. Perhaps they were afraid if they got too close to the ED teacher, they might be assigned ED students in the future. Or, maybe, it was a school in which relationships among staff members were not valued.

When I attended the special education meetings, I heard war stories of the burnout rate among us. I wonder, now, if that had more to do with the lack of a support system than the difficulty of the job. Don't get me wrong—teaching is incredibly hard work, and I lay awake nights trying to figure out how to handle a particularly difficult behavior issue many times. But, as I said, I didn't know many people in my school. The school had a culture of cliques, but not a widespread caring feel for everyone.

Fast-forward to my last school in Florida, at which I was a guidance counselor for 6½ years before becoming the principal for 7 years before moving to Arizona. The feel of the school was palpable, to me when I walked in the first time, to new staff members I hired, to new families who came to our school from all over the country, and to business folks who came in the school to do business. After learning the names of the 500 students at the school, I used to joke that our school was a lot like *Cheers* without the bar, of course. It's a place where everyone knew your name and knew where you had vacationed last and knew the names of all your kids who attended the school 10 years ago. In other words, it was like being a part of a family.

In a book of teacher interviews about working in abusive environments, Schnall (2009) has an entire section devoted to the feeling of being supported, or not. And in surveying teachers about trust, teachers said they either felt supported or not in their schools. What does support look like and feel like? Many surveyed teachers indicated they trusted principals more when they backed up the teacher, no matter what. But some also said things like standing up for the teacher in the face of adversity or having the teachers' backs until proven otherwise. "Being on our side" and "sticking up for teachers" were other comments that were made by multiple teachers. Other phrases included "supportive," "praising," and "being loyal to staff."

Everyone wants to feel support in their work. Rath and Clifton (2004) in their book *How Full is Your Bucket* speak about how, in the Korean War, the North Koreans kept prisoners from giving each other emotional support, but rather encouraged and rewarded informants and snitches. The intent was to break up relationships and turn the prisoners against one another. Support is an incredibly strong force, one that makes a system powerful and mighty. Without support and encouragement, the system breaks down. Buckets are drained and negativity abounds. But Clifton and his peers decided to study the flipside of this terrible situation. They pondered: If people can be devastated and destroyed by negative reinforcement, can the opposite happen? Can they be inspired by the same degree of positivity?

I think the trust research would indicate an affirmative answer. Time after time, in survey after survey complete with anecdotal and qualitative remarks, teachers indicated they trusted more and enjoyed work more when they felt supported in their school environment. But support goes far beyond simple recognition and praise

(Rath & Clifton, 2004), although even recognition and praise can increase productivity, increase engagement, encourage longevity with a company/school, increase higher satisfaction scores from customers, and improve attendance.

Teachers want a principal to be visible (Arneson, 2012; Schnall, 2009), but this doesn't mean the principal is visiting classrooms to spy on teachers or to catch them performing inadequately. Ken Blanchard, author of the *One-Minute Manager,* says he stops by his companies' offices simply to energize people who work for him. Principals want teachers to be visible, as well. In addition to being seen in the hallways for hall duty and in the lunchroom and on the bus ramp to monitor students, most principals want to see teachers stop by their office, if only to say hi. One of my very favorite parts of being a principal was knowing staff members would randomly pop in just to say hi or to tell me the latest adorably funny kid story. When we first adopted the seven habits of leadership (Covey, 1989) into our school repertoire, I had a puppet on my news show talk to all the kids about synergizing. "It means working as a team and getting more done because we all worked together." Later that week, one of the kindergarten teachers popped her head in my office as the students were headed out to P.E. "James, tell Mrs. Arneson what you said about cleaning up before we left for P.E." James stepped forward and said, "I can't thtand cleaning, but we thenergithzed and it ith thpick and thpan in our clathroom now." Priceless!!!

E-Cubed: Effective Evaluation Example

What is your most recent favorite kid story?

With whom have you shared it?

Stories from our work often energize us and bond us. Share a "good news" story today from your work.

Here's something else I have discovered. You can't say you believe in something and then not do it in practice. At least not for very long. We read a verse in the Bible a few weeks ago from James 3:11. In essence, it says a fountain cannot yield both salt water and fresh water. To me, this speaks to our characters, as educators and as human beings. If we say we are going to be supportive in one breath, we can't then be vindictive to one another in the next breath. But I've heard many people say this is exactly how their schools operate.

> "I like the people I work with—they don't bother me and I don't bother them."

> "I wish I could share ideas with my grade-level teachers. They just don't seem receptive to new ideas."

> "I'm not sure if I can trust whose side anyone is on in this school."

> "She says one thing, but I watch her do something else entirely."

When I was talking to another consultant, recently, about school climate, she asked me, "What traditions in your school promoted support?" I laughed out loud before I answered, "We ate together—a lot." There is something about food that brings us together in fellowship. What happens when we break bread together? We also ask, "Where did you get this recipe?" (My answer used to be "a la Sam's Club" until I saw the true value in bringing something homemade to share with the people with whom I worked). In eating homemade dishes together, we discover new information about families, traditions, and interests that might otherwise go undiscovered. Setting up and cleaning up for a get-together can also be tremendously bonding for a faculty and staff willing to put the work into it. Our school even put together a recipe book to sell as a fundraiser, documenting our love for cooking and sharing good food.

Other folks, when asked what makes their school environment seem supportive, cite the following:

> "When another teacher shares an idea, we all jump to write it down right away. After all, it's something we might be able to use ourselves later on."

> "At the beginning of the day, the principal and staff all greet each other in a caring, loving way. If I have to be away from my family, this is where I want to be."

> "Parents feel like they are a part of the culture here, not intruding into someone else's territory."

"I've worked in other schools where you wondered whose side people were on. Here, we are on the side of the kids and everything else follows."

In which situation would you rather work? It's a rhetorical question, right? When people feel supported, more good things get done. When a school has this supportive feel, it bleeds into the classroom and the students feel it. Less discipline problems arise. More time can be spent on the business of schools, which is teaching and learning.

When adults cannot get along or have disagreements, the students feel it. But they shouldn't. If we have a concern or disagreement with another staff member, this should be taken care of in private, and dirty laundry should be kept in the laundry room. Unfortunately, this doesn't always happen, and it doesn't take too long for a pattern of disrespect or foul language to become ballpark talk in the community. Websites like Greatschools.com are places in which parents and community can and will vent about the professionalism seen in schools. We need to make sure we put our best foot forward in public and address the elephants in the room in private.

Support is the foundation for getting through difficult times, whether it is work related (i.e., a difficult parent conference, behavior issues in the classroom) or at home (a child is sneaking out at night, the family dog just passed away). Support is much like fresh air. We may take it for granted if we have it, but it will be extremely difficult to catch a good breath when we don't feel it or if we feel the antithesis of it.

When one of the teachers at our school developed cancer in her brain, she would come in my office on an ongoing basis and break down in tears, unsure of what direction to go with medical insurance, etc. As we worked through those logistics, she began coming in my office even more often to break down in tears. "I just am overwhelmed at all the support I feel here," she would say.

Support and honesty will go far toward creating the type of climate that promotes trust among teachers and principals, maximizing the effectiveness of the evaluation process.

CHAPTER NINE

Factors Influencing Trust and Communication

> *If you want one year of prosperity, grow grain. If you want 10 years of prosperity, grow trees. If you want 100 years of prosperity, grow people.*
>
> —Chinese proverb

W hat does good communication look like and what influences it? In examining more closely the barriers to trust and communication from the research (Arneson, 2012), the top 10 included:

- Letting employees be the last to know
- Not responding to emails or phone calls
- Lack of open communication
- Closed doors
- Not listening
- No communication after walkthroughs
- Poor communication skills
- Withholding information
- Ineffective communicators
- Inability to openly discuss concerns

Let's take a look at them again and define how each relates to the evaluation process.

1. *Letting employees be the last to know:* Teachers do not want to hear a vital piece of information related to the observation/ evaluation process from other teachers in the school or other schools in the district. Information shared as quickly as possible will enhance the feeling of collaboration.

2. *Not responding to emails or phone calls:* As much as principals ask teachers to keep parents informed, teachers don't always believe principals are timely in their feedback, especially returning lesson plans that were due or sending evidence collected from the observation. A related concern involves principals conducting walkthroughs and not giving teachers feedback. One school system with whom I worked put a time limit on responding to emails (i.e., "Staff members should all check and respond to emails by the end of the school day," the policy stated). When interviewed for a job as a professor at an online university, I was asked the very question, "What time frame is reasonable, in your opinion, to get back with students who have questions?"

   The problem with this stipulation is that some people feel it micromanages them. Common sense should tell us that, out of respect for another person, we should respond to them within a reasonable timeframe. After all, if we want good customer service ourselves, which we all do, we should give the same courtesy to those with whom we work. Particularly when the teacher pay is contingent upon the feedback and final evaluation by the supervisor, tensions are likely to rise when timely feedback is not maintained.

3. *Lack of open or effective communication:* Teachers express concern about the lack of good communication and, many times, even expressed concern that the principal may be unable to communicate effectively. If a principal doesn't share their thoughts on the observed lesson or is unable to reflect effectively about ways for the teacher to improve, how shall the teacher trust their instructional leader? Along the same lines, communicating effectively is now part of most teacher evaluations. If teachers are not able to communicate effectively with their students, how in the world can we expect that they

will be able to do the same with their peers or supervisors? Take, for example, a teacher who finishes giving instructions and opening content to a lesson and she reflects, later, to her principal or peers, "It was such a great lesson," all the while not taking note of the 14 out of 18 confused looks on student faces. Or perhaps the student talk that ensues immediately after she is finished, "What did she say to do?" "What did that mean?" Just listening to ourselves speak can often clear up any confusing habits we may have when speaking to others. I once asked a colleague to monitor my directions to the participants in a workshop for any confusion. Getting feedback from an objective party can be quite helpful if you are willing to accept the feedback.

E-Cubed: Effective Evaluation Example

Consider asking a fellow administrator or other trusted colleague to give you feedback on your communication skills in meetings, workshops, or even in person.

---

4. *Closed doors:* Open doors invite trust. Closed doors solidify concerns of mistrust. While pre- and post-observation conferences should take place behind closed doors, on how many other occasions is the principal's door shut? On a school staff, if there are three or four teachers who seem to gather in one classroom and talk privately on an ongoing basis, other staff members may begin to feel a bit of mistrust. Cliques or secretive talk can make for sure signs of a lack of trust in schools and need to be flushed out.

5. *Not listening and other poor communication skills:* As Charlotte Danielson so eloquently points out in one of her interviews about post-observation conferences, how must a teacher feel when he or she simply must endure the principal's assessment of the lesson observed before being dismissed without a chance to reflect openly about the lesson that very teacher taught? When teachers have the ability to do a good bit of the talking in a post-observation conference, and are able to openly reflect on their teaching in a safe and trusting

environment, true growth is likely to take place, even in the newest and least experienced of teachers.

SHARED LEADERSHIP

Throughout the research on trust (Arneson, 2012), participants also indicated some barriers to trusting the leadership in their school. One barrier was about micromanaging and not sharing leadership opportunities. Anecdotal comments expressed about barriers to trust in administrators included the following:

- Not knowing how to delegate
- Micromanaging
- Exclusion of stakeholders
- Nitpicks things
- Being heavy handed
- Controlling
- Never asking for input
- Not willing to try new ideas

A principal new to his school said he was inundated with comments such as "We always do it this way" and "Aren't you going to do this event like our former principal did?" The principal said, by October, he was ready to pull his hair out and scream, "I'm NOT the former principal and I'll do it whatever way I want!" Sounds familiar to teachers who have ever substitute taught. Inevitably, students will say, "We pass our papers this way when Ms. Morris is here" to which the frustrated substitute finally wants to scream "Well, I'm NOT Ms. Morris, am I?" That's what we might want to say, but we are professionals and don't talk like that.

Certainly, educators across the country are feeling the growing pains of "That's not the way we have always conducted teacher observations and evaluations." Reina and Reina (2006) call this phenomenon *contractual trust*. Contractual trust implies that people have a mutual understanding that they will do what they say they individually will do. "That's the way we always did it before" can fall in this category. The key, it would seem, to building contractual trust is the issue of knowing the expectations of all the parties involved and keeping one's word in inherent or expected agreements. Reina and

Reina (2006) say that keeping agreements, another essential element of contractual trust, "speaks to an individual's and an organization's reliability in carrying out their commitments" (p. 28). In other words, when we keep agreements, we empower our relationships and build trust between ourselves and others.

When I first became principal, the teachers quickly informed me that we always wore jeans on Friday and we always got to leave right after dismissal on Friday. Some things I could live with, I thought, as I decided that casual Fridays weren't such a bad thing. But early dismissal every Friday? That seemed to preclude anyone ever meeting with parents (or with me, for that matter) on a Friday. I talked with the faculty and agreed that, while not every Friday could be "leave early Friday," I would make an announcement on periodic Fridays that folks were free to get their work done in an alternate location once all their school commitments had been fulfilled. While some folks still felt for a few months as though I had pulled the "free Friday" out from underneath them, they seemed to understand the reasoning in that not being a contractual expectation.

SHARED DECISION MAKING

The power of shared decision making is cyclical in nature. The more we share decision making, the more staff members feel empowered, the easier the decision making will be in the future.

Principals who allow teachers into the behind-the-scenes processes of the school will avoid looking like the Great and Powerful Oz. "Pay no attention to the man behind the curtain" need not be the order of the day. The truth is, many staff members would rather not be involved in the inner workings of the budget or the daily grind of assigning custodial and maintenance tasks. But the power in asking and allowing interested parties to participate in shared leadership is undeniable. Take, for instance, a school that has traditionally been run mainly by the principal. Each year, the budget is surreptitiously completed with a wave of a magic wand (maybe not, but definitely done behind closed doors and solely by the principal). One year, the principal (perhaps a new leader to the school) announces one day at a staff meeting, "I will be working on the budget for next year in the next week. I am passing out a survey so you can indicate the priority you place on certain programs, amenities, and positions in our school. This Thursday, I will be going through the budget piece by piece in the conference room. If anyone would like to join me for an in-depth look at how the money is generated, how much we are allocated for certain programs, how we are funded, and how we might best use our resources, I invite you to join me."

What just happened? A bit of the mystique has been removed from the process, first of all, and a task that has typically been completed in a unilateral fashion is now becoming more collaborative. The proverbial curtain has been drawn from the inner workings of Oz.

The first year I invited collaboration, several people attended, asked questions, and were in awe of what all is entailed in the budget process. Not only was the veil lifted, but perhaps even a bit of respect for the cumbersome, tedious task involved was experienced. The next year, a couple of people came but others said, "I'm glad you are good at that and enjoy it but I trust that you will do what is best for the school." Interesting, since several had mentioned a lack of trust in the budget process before that time. Perhaps lifting the veil and making it more of an open-kimono process was helpful in more ways than one. Another principal I know used to say, "Nobody would want to do what I have to do" about the budget or hiring teachers or whatever, without the same satisfied results. It seems we can't be *told* we wouldn't want to be a part of a collaborative process but rather should have the option to participate then make a decision of whether it is an interest that is in our wheelhouse or not.

If staff find it empowering to be involved in decision making at various levels, it might be interesting to ask how rules (rights, responsibilities, routines, and procedures) are determined in a classroom. Does the teacher who is vehement about being involved in the process of creating a duty schedule have the same vehemence of sharing decision making in the classroom?

E-Cubed: Effective Evaluation Example

How are decisions at your school and in your district made?

Are there any unilateral decisions that could become shared decisions?

What about in the classroom? How are rights and responsibilities determined? By the teacher or with student input?

How is the schedule for duties made in your school or district? In some counties or districts, it is often stated in a master contract that a schedule should be "approved" by a committee. But in most schools in which I have worked, that means the principal or assistant principal designs the schedule and then it is handed to the committee or the entire staff to put their rubber stamp of approval on it. Scheduling, however, is one of the biggest time consumers to school administrators, and in most cases, the school administrator is the one to whom the schedule of duties matters the least. All areas simply need to be covered, is the underlying feeling. To whom does the duty schedule matter the most? Staff members. So, why not have a committee to make the duty schedule, being certain to represent all areas, grade levels, and departments in the school?

Reciprocal process. Allowing a reciprocal process for shared leadership means decisions are not unilateral nor are principals considered the only experts in leadership and teachers considered the only experts in instruction. Sharing and even changing up roles can be a powerful method for encouraging increased trust in a school.

Who leads faculty meetings? Typically the building principal. But what happens if the main topic needing to be addressed is about the upcoming Kids' Vote event next week? Why not have the media specialist and his committee be the bulk of the meeting to encourage participation and democracy. On the flipside, who typically teaches workshops to the faculty on instructional techniques (new evaluation, Common Core strategies, etc.)? In many schools, this task is conducted by an outside presenter or the instructional coach. If the principal of a school is going to be viewed as the true instructional leader in the school and not simply the manager of facilities and personnel, my hunch is he or she needs to deliver professional development, at least some of the time. My experience after we adopted the Danielson Framework for Teacher Effectiveness was one of role modeling and demonstrating the techniques I now expected we should see in the classroom. And, along with that, I demonstrated my strengths and areas of improvement in teaching. While establishing respect and rapport is a forte of mine, there were times when the technology would go awry and I would say, "This might not be the best example of managing my resources. I need to make sure I am able to demonstrate flexibility and responsiveness if the technology messes up." It's what I expect to happen in the classroom. Teachers appreciate their school leaders role-modeling their expertise and their imperfections, as well.

Build Capacity

While some administrators relish in telling their teachers, "You would hate doing what I have to do every day," I fear this is possibly the antithesis of growing capacity. Same premise with teachers. If you have a practicum student or student teacher, are you always giving them the doom and gloom of being a teacher, or are you sharing the ah-ha moments that are likely the reason we keep coming back to the classroom every day or every year? If all we do is scare people off from the profession of teaching or leadership, what will our schools look like in 5 years? Ten years? I prefer, instead, to mentor aspiring teachers and aspiring administrators with a well-balanced view of the profession, along with multiple opportunities for participation and reflection. Let's be honest. There are several things we can say to ward potential teachers away from this profession. Low pay, new accountability, pay based on student test scores, and other issues in education can seem quite intimidating. But how do we compare those paradigm shifts to the sense of satisfaction experienced when a student who had previously shown little or no interest in reading all of a sudden has a light bulb breakthrough? No comparison, right?

E-Cubed: Effective Evaluation Example

What keeps you motivated to stay in the field of education?

Think back to a time in which a student or an aspiring teacher experienced an ah-ha moment in your presence. How did it feel?

Another way in which we build capacity is in hiring new teachers. What is the process by which your school interviews and hires new teachers? When I was a teacher in Texas, New Mexico, and Florida, teachers were either hired by the central office and then assigned to a particular school or, once hired, the teacher got to go visit school principals until a "love connection" was made. As an administrator, I was excited about the interview and hiring process but also recognized that the teachers on the grade level would have a tremendous vested interest in what kind of teacher we hired. So, with each new opening, I invited the grade-level chair and maybe one other teacher from the grade level to sit in on the interviews. We met ahead of time to generate pertinent questions (we had a general template but, depending on the grade level and special needs of the position, the questions could be tweaked to be more appropriate) and to address any anxiety on the part of the interviewers. Some teachers talked about how they had never done anything like this before, and they were nervous themselves. Others expressed delight in, for once, being a part of a process that impacted them so much. We agreed to individually rate each candidate on a scale of 1–5 or 1–10 (I like to do 1–10 if we have more than three or four candidates) after each asking the candidates a pre-designated question or two.

The process felt so collaborative, the chosen candidate felt like a new member of our family. Everyone agreed if there was a tie, I would make the final decision. For that reason, once we had made a decision, we would either call the teacher together or, as a favorite tradition we started, the interview team would hop in my car and drive to the teacher's house with flowers or a school t-shirt or a current book we were tackling for a book study and invite them to be a part of our school community. Every candidate chosen mentioned the camaraderie they felt in this process. "I already feel as though I am part of a team" was the general theme of the comments expressed. Imagine how much more enhanced every piece of the evaluation process will be when this type of trust and communication are established and nurtured.

CHARACTER AND COMPETENCE

Before embarking on trust research, I had read multiple books about trust, including Stephen M. R. Covey's book *The Speed of Trust*. He said he believed trust in organizations was based upon four cores of credibility: Integrity, Intent, Capabilities, and Results. He indicated he believed these four cores play equally into someone's trust or mistrust of us. I wondered if teacher trust in principals would lean more toward one than the other. For the sake of simplicity, I combined cores into two facets, competence and character. Competence would entail capabilities and results (was the leader capable of leading a school and producing results necessary to mark a successful school?). Character would encompass the leader's integrity and general intentions toward stakeholders in the school.

The instrument primarily used to measure teacher trust in studying trust was the Omnibus Trust Scale (Hoy & Tschannen-Moran, 2003). In this research, the principals' competence ranked higher in this research (4.98 average) than the character (4.66 average). I also examined the beliefs of the 100 participants who indicated they had the "highest" degree of trust in their principal. Again, the difference between trust in character versus trust in competence was minimal enough for me to conclude that character and competence were valued to much the same degree.

E-Cubed: Effective Evaluation Example

What is your level of trust in your direct supervisor?
With your colleagues?

What matters more to you—character or competence?

Reina and Reina (2006) talk about competence trust in depth. They define it as "Trust of Capability." Competence trust is an absolute requirement for work to get done effectively. Narrowly speaking, it means being able to rely on someone to complete a specific task. While speaking with teachers in a district in the northeast United States this winter, three teachers got on the subject of their own principal. They said, "He is such a nice person, but he is not at all effective or qualified to handle this job." When that feeling is prevalent among staff members, it is difficult to make progress. In fact, without trust, progress is deterred in a corporation. The question is, "In deciding whether or not to trust someone, should I go with my head or my heart?"

Reina and Reina (n.d.) talk about the dual direction of trust. While most of my own research primarily focused on teacher trust in the principal, Reina and Reina talk about a leader's trust in the team members and even in ourselves:

As Sylvia Hernandez, executive director of a national sales association, comments, "When I trust the skills and abilities of my team, it allows them to trust in their potential competence. It actually provides them with a remarkable gift. When I trust in them, it opens the door for them to trust in themselves. I have learned that in order to trust in the competence of others, I have to trust in my own competence."

It seems that trust in others can actually boost productivity and that cyclical effect of trust in schools. Take, for example, this quote by Henry L. Stimson (n.d.), former U.S. Secretary of State: "The chief lesson I have learned in a long life is that the only way to make a man trustworthy is to trust him; and the surest way to make him untrustworthy is to distrust him and show your distrust."

For me, this goes back to building capacity. If schools believe each person, that is every person, has innate abilities on which we can draw strength, the system of the school seems to operate at a much more effective rate. But one might argue: Are we going to entrust someone to do a job if they aren't prepared to do it, just so we can lift their spirits? Of course not. We trust smartly. The point is, we have to find strengths of each other, so we aren't micromanaging everything in the name of "I'm the only one competent enough to handle this task."

How can we build this climate of competence trust in our buildings? I propose a five-fold process.

Few things can help an individual more than to place responsibility on him, and to let him know that you trust him.

—Booker T. Washington

1. *Find out people's strengths.* Our school's parent-teacher organization did something that helped with this a few years ago. The five people who held offices were a bit disgruntled and tired of doing the heavy lifting for every single fund-raising event. They designed a questionnaire that would be filled out at our back-to-school Open House. The form basically asked, "What are you good at? What services can you provide to our school?" They collected all the responses and put together a book of skills our community members possessed. Some were the people's businesses (Mr. Clark owned his own copy shop; Mrs. Simms was a seamstress by trade); others were simply their hobbies (Mrs. Gibson was great at designing t-shirts; Mr. Patel's pastries were coveted by all). Not only did this

endeavor distribute work more equitably among the community, it also made people appreciate one another to a much greater extent.

2. *Be willing to help build skills in others.* We've all witnessed the situation in which someone struggles with a task (maybe logging on and using a new website), only to have someone come over and take over for them ("Here, let me do that for you"). While it might seem nice, the helper has sufficiently just eliminated an opportunity for learning. It's precisely what we don't want our students in class to do. "Help him work through and reason through the problem but don't give him the answer." We need to help others build their skills. Competence trust is based on the belief that other people might be worthy of developing new skill sets.

3. *Plan for the sharing of information and ideas.* Sharing ideas and new information does not come naturally for some people. We may have to set up scenarios to make this happen. I liken this to the idea of lesson study. Many will say, "Our grade level has been sharing lesson plans for years. This lesson study stuff is nothing new," then come to find out what sharing meant was they would give each other copies of things they had done in the past. Lesson study puts the sharing of ideas on steroids and plans opportunities to chew on those ideas before developing a new or revised plan.

4. *Be willing to brainstorm solutions to problem areas.* Brainstorming new ideas within a group involves open mindedness. Reina and Reina (2006) say one indication of a low-trust environment is the "not-invented-here" syndrome. People exhibiting this syndrome will ignore or discount suggestions of others simply because they didn't think of them first. We have to make sure we leverage each other's competencies.

5. *Celebrate successes of one another.* As mentioned in the previous chapter, support for one another goes an incredibly long way to building trust among staff members. We need to know if people are amenable to accepting praise and recognition in a group setting or whether they prefer to be recognized privately, but once the method is known, let's celebrate new

skill sets being developed. When we began the school year last year, we had an award made. It was simply a chunk of rock on a wood base, with the inscription "You ROCK!" The "You ROCK" award was initially awarded to Pam Willard, who designed our school t-shirts for that year. While everyone knew Pam was talented, many didn't know she possessed that skill set. The unique thing about the "You ROCK" award is that you can continue to pass it around. Perhaps the person who is awarded the rock can be on the lookout for the next recipient, someone who goes outside his or her comfort zone to develop or hone a new skill.

BUILDING CHARACTER TRUST

In workshops, I ask participants to picture one person with whom they work and with whom they have a high degree of trust. When we talk more in-depth about what qualities people use in determining whether or not they will give their trust to someone, people often say, "Their actions are consistent with what they say they are going to do." Integrity is all about what we do, even when no one is watching us. If I tell a teacher I will hold their information in confidentiality, and then go spread the news, I am not acting with integrity, even if it never gets back to the original person. The point in this scenario is, if I am going to spread someone else's laundry to the world, what is going to convince the world I won't do the same with their laundry? Other people, in speaking of why they trust someone, say comments such as:

"She makes ethical decisions."

"He treats me the same way he treats everyone else."

"I don't ever feel sabotaged by this person."

Think of someone with whom you have a high-trust relationship. What does it look like? What does it feel like? What is the communication like? How enjoyable is your relationship? The fact of the matter is: When we trust someone's character, everything is made easier. Covey (2006) says everything works better with trust. He quotes Jim Burke, Former Chairman and CEO of Johnson and Johnson:

You can't have success without trust. The word trust embodies almost everything you can strive for that will help you to succeed. You tell me any human relationship that works without trust, whether it is a marriage or a friendship or a social interaction; in the long run, the same is true about business, especially businesses that deal with the public. (p. 6)

The problem with character trust is we can't rest on our laurels. In other words, we can't hide behind the past, even if we believe we were trusted once. School staff members must continuously strive to maintain and improve trusting relationships between one another. Consider the trust with others a sacred entity and treat it as such at all times.

The ways we can increase character trust in schools is three-fold.

1. *Act with integrity.* Always ask these questions before speaking of someone else: *Is it true? Is it kind? Is it necessary to say?* If the answer to any of those questions is no, then it is probably gossip and should likely be avoided.

2. *Stick with the winners.* If I want to be considered trustworthy, I should likely consider with whom I am spending the bulk of my time. A teacher once said to me, "I want to try to be nice to everyone, but I just know I need to stick mostly with people who are going to speak kindly about other people."

3. *Forgive minor errors and be willing to move past them.* If you have put your trust in someone, and they make an error in judgment, consider forgiveness. A principal I know got called a name by his superintendent. Totally inappropriate, of course. There truly is no excuse for name calling in our profession. However, he was able to come back after the superintendent apologized for his inappropriate language and say, "This was an anomaly. I forgive my boss" and move past it.

The factors contributing to high levels of trust, including communication, shared leadership and shared decision making, character, and competence have an enormous potential for impacting how teachers will view the evaluation process.

CHAPTER TEN

The Legacy We Leave Behind

No legacy is so rich as honesty.

—William Shakespeare

Schools need to expect to see the climate they wish to see, and it will likely happen, much more so than if we simply hope it will change. This is akin to Cesar Millan's theory of dog training. No, I'm not talking about the idea of doing an alpha dog roll in which you pin children to the ground. What I mean is that Cesar expects the dogs he trains to behave better because he has taught them exactly what he wants them to do. When Cesar demonstrates that confident air that he has taught the behavior and now he should see it, the desired behaviors are displayed. I certainly see many differences between canines and those with whom we work, but the fact remains that we must do the following to get the desired behaviors:

1. Agree upon the behavior we want to see.

2. Communicate the desired behavior to all stakeholders.

3. Expect the desired behavior to take hold.

4. Inspect the school for the desired behavior.

5. Praise everyone demonstrating the desired behavior.

One of the keys to the above plan (Arneson, 2011a) is that we must inspect what we expect. Many great leaders have shared this theory of running companies. If we expect a particular behavior, we need to be willing to watch for it happening and point it out when it does. This goes for teachers in the classroom or principals in the office.

Rath and Clifton (2004) say one of the best ways we can fill each other's buckets is to get to know each other better. Building a climate of support in schools starts with recognizing we are all in this together and, thus, we need to support one another. If we maintain the stance that we are terminally unique, we'll simply walk around feeling like nobody can understand how hard we have it. You know what I mean: A new initiative is brought up and a teacher says, "Oh but that would never work in my classroom." A principal throws out a great idea during a district meeting and two other principals say, "We could never do that in our schools. Our children are different on this side of town." The problem with terminal uniqueness is exacerbated in the observation/evaluation process. Kindergarten teachers will initially look at the evaluation instrument and say, "My students don't do the same type of questioning skills that twelfth graders do. I should have a different instrument on which to be evaluated." Likewise, teachers of students with special needs might say, "My students can't show that level of engagement." The truly unique thing I have found in being a school leader and educational consultant is that every teacher does have the capacity to teach well. Good teaching is good teaching, whether we are in a twelfth-grade economics class or a kindergarten class with students with special needs. I have watched, time and time again, excellent teaching that encompasses every piece of the evaluation instrument.

On the flipside, if we recognize we are in the boat with other folks who are trying to row the same direction, we may be able to get somewhere. Instead of looking at differences, we will be amazed at how similar we are and how beneficial the ideas of others are to us if we but open our minds to the possibilities.

Schools can build this climate of mutual support in several ways, including:

1. Work together, eat together, and play together.

2. Build each other up without tearing each other down.

3. Recognizing that this is not an episode of *Survivor*—no one needs to get voted off the island.

4. Recognize everyone's need to vent . . . but vent in small doses.

5. Remember who wins if support is there. Remember who loses if support is not there.

Let's take a look at the nature of this support, one strategy at a time.

1. WORK TOGETHER, EAT TOGETHER, AND PLAY TOGETHER

One of the most time-consuming things we did at our elementary school was our Spring Fling. You know the drill. Spring festival, complete with bounce houses, cake walks, games, and concessions. While our amazing parent-teacher organization members did the bulk of the work, truly, we all had set-up and take down to do for our area. As a principal, I usually manned a grill, cooking burgers and hot dogs and calling out, "Come and get it! Get your hot dog!" for 2 or 3 hours, at which time I smelled like something that was going to attract all the dogs in the neighborhood. And, my voice was shot. When the event was over, however, there was much cleanup and money counting to do before we could call it a night. As much as I hate to admit this because we were falling down exhausted by then, this was my favorite time of the night. Staff members and parents joined together in the clean-up, exhaustion had turned to delusional, giddy, slap-happy sillies. Nothing was funny, but we laughed at everything. We sang songs and danced in the hallway. We were working together to get the school cleaned back up after a night that the whole community had enjoyed. The key? We were all working hard for a common goal. Anyone who has ever gone on a mission trip or done long days of volunteer work knows this phenomenon. When we work hard together, it bonds us. Who knew sweat was the glue that binds us together?

Bonding will add to the sense of trust between and among faculty members. So how can we recreate that without having a Fall Festival or Spring Fling every week? The short answer is, you can't, although we always had fun reliving some of the more fun moments through pictures and inside jokes long after the night was over. But on a smaller scale, how about assigning a task at each faculty meeting in which teams must work together to complete a small project? It is important to make sure it is not just busy work and that it has a purpose, and it is equally important to make the task something teachers can then say, "Ooh, I could do something like this in my classroom." When in doubt, make all information relevant and applicable to attendees' work.

As for eating together, there are many ways to build this in to a school routine. One idea is to have an "eat and greet" every time there is a birthday or special day. Not so surprisingly, the talk for the first 15 minutes of our get-together sounded something like, "Oh my gosh, who made this great dip?" to which another teacher would reply, "Oh that was Jane. She makes that every time we have a pot-luck because we all request it. It is a handed-down recipe from her grandmother, who used to teach here." And so it went, people sharing food and sharing stories and ultimately building relationships. I'm aware that schools are almost always a place in which people bring in food and leave it in the lounge for the staff to eat when they come in for a cup of coffee. But leaving food to be eaten in the lounge is not the same thing as sharing a meal together. Maria, a dear friend from my last school, used to say, "Fellowship around food is the best kind. When we break bread together, we also break down walls of hurt." So very true!

Obviously, we are in schools to work for and with our students. They are the reason we are there. In order to be the very best we can be, however, we need to take time to laugh and have fun. "All work and no play makes Jack a dull boy," right? There are those who have no interest in socializing outside the school day with other staff members. And there are those who might say the principal has no business becoming friendly with the staff. I respect the rights of those who don't want to come to Happy Hours after school, and many folks have family commitments that prevent them from joining in the fun. The year I became a principal, a new P.E. teacher came to our school. He was young, energetic, and hilarious. Lance brought a new joie de vivre to our school, which had never been lacking in joy to begin with. That year, we began meeting for Happy Hour every couple of weeks. I would go for a little while and then slip out and let the staff enjoy time without "the boss" there. I don't think most folks cared one way or the other, I'm simply not that important, but it mattered to me to balance being there with not being too much there. Plus, what if their venting needed to be a bit about their boss? In order to build trust, principals and staff need to recognize the elephant in the room of venting. We all need a chance to blow off steam without getting defensive and fearful.

And what about those who can't get to an off-site get together? Fun can be made during the school day as well. And there are always people who get things going. Theresa was our spiritual guidance at my last school. She would put little verses in staff boxes to brighten people's days. It must be said that she would also occasionally put a pair of panties (from our children's clothing donation box for just-in-case-of-accidents) in a staff member's box with a note saying, "Did you lose these somewhere?" Another staff member loves practical jokes. She put a sign on the copy machine that said, "The copy machine is now voice activated. Simply say how many copies you need and tell it to start and it will begin." The ensuing spectacle was priceless. The best part, she said, was watching a teacher stand there and say, "I need 25 copies, please. (pause) I said 25 copies. (pause) This thing is not working at all for me."

Laughter surely is the best medicine, and it is such a necessary ingredient in a somewhat stressful job. I like to ask people to recall the last time they laughed at their school or at their place of employment. Sadly, many people say they go weeks or months without laughing. I don't think we can afford to do that.

2. Build each other up without
Tearing each other down

Supporting each other includes recognizing each other's strengths and celebrating them without feeling threatened by them. Why is it that, in some schools, an expert in math instruction could teach math workshops in every other school in the district with rave reviews, but arms would remain folded when that same person teaches in their own school? Why cannot a teacher be considered a prophet in his or her own land? Perhaps it has much to do with the inherent competitive nature of teachers. I have worked in schools in which this phenomenon is more present than others. One superintendent told me recently that she would like me to come do the

Danielson training in her district versus having her own staff conduct the training, simply because she felt the teachers would be more receptive to an outsider. How could that be? We work in one of the most caring professions of all. How could we not support another, one of our own, standing in front of us to present material we need to be taught? Perhaps, again, it is because educators are tough on ourselves and watching one of our own teach us makes us hold a measuring stick to ourselves and wonder, "Am I doing enough?" or "Am I as good as he is?"

3. THIS IS NOT *SURVIVOR*—NO ONE
NEEDS TO GET VOTED OFF THE ISLAND

Being supportive, however, means remembering one very important fact. We are in this profession for one reason: to help students become their best possible selves. We also must remember that this goal is not like a season of *Survivor.* No one has to get voted off the island in order to win. In fact, winning becomes much easier when we work together for the common good.

I was talking with a group of principals in Arizona the other day, and we got on the topic of praise, recognition, and sharing of ideas. Someone talked about how their staff wasn't able to share ideas very well because if someone said, "Oh I tried something in my classroom I wanted to share," others would cross their arms and figure out a way to not like the idea . . . or, worse yet, the person. Todd Whitaker (2008) talks about superstar teachers, those who represent maybe 10% of the faculty in a school. He makes the distinction that these teachers can't be perceived as the principal's pet but must be perceived well by all members of the faculty. Whitaker says superstar teachers want autonomy and recognition, a balance that can be difficult to achieve. They want to be able to do what they know to be best practice for students and also be recognized for those efforts in an appropriate manner.

The goal, of course, is to be able to build up superstars in our schools without the perception of those teachers being the principal's favorite and one whom is lifted up as a deity at every faculty meeting. For example, the principal asks Frank to share an idea he did using Venn diagrams in that morning's lesson. Frank talks and people listen. Like E.F. Hutton, all is quiet when Frank speaks. Teachers ask questions, take notes, and quickly figure out how they can adapt Frank's idea to their own classroom. What happens, though, if Frank is the only one asked to share ideas at the faculty meetings? What happens if Frank begins thinking he has an idea for everything and shares every one, negating the ever-important equity of voice? Frank will become a pariah. When he speaks, people will roll their eyes and say (to themselves or even out loud, in some cases), "Oh no, there he goes again."

The culture for learning in a classroom is critical to the respect and rapport students feel and give for one another. The same can be said of the culture for learning in a school. If a faculty truly respects the accomplishments, thoughts, and ideas of each member, the group collectively gets better and better. One way to do this is through sharing days. We used to have what we called "Thinking Thursdays." The premise behind these sharing times was that anyone and everyone had great ideas to share. Each week, someone would sign up to host a Thinking Thursday in their classroom. The location was important because the climate was about sharing in and from the classroom. Mrs. Banks volunteered for one Thursday and demonstrated how she was using hula-hoops to teach Venn diagrams. Each participant got a pair of hula-hoops. Mrs. Banks had snacks in her room, and folks signed up to come and listen and discuss for one hour after school. The sharing was informal, casual, and mostly gave folks a chance to see Mrs. Banks' room and other ideas she had. Several teachers filled up pages in their notebooks with ideas from just sitting with other teachers in a room all set up with great ideas.

As an administrator, I realized this was a chance to see there was not just one person with great ideas on the faculty. Instead, several people shared innovative ideas that sparked others to be creative and innovative as well. And that, I believe, is one of the true aims of a building of trust—safety in sharing different ideas and perspectives.

E-Cubed: Effective Evaluation Example

Ask a teacher leader to host a Thinking Thursday. Invite them to share a teaching strategy or fun idea with their colleagues. It is best to have them host in their classroom so teachers can also look at how the idea is used within the room.

4. Recognize everyone's need
to vent . . . but vent in small doses

During the first couple of years I was a principal, I realized one of my weaker areas—I was fearful of controversy. While hundreds of parents would express their love for a school that had very little tension, one parent was honest in saying, "I had a problem this year, but I didn't want to come to you with it." "Oh no!" I cried. "Why didn't you bring it to me?" She said, "Everything always seems so perfect here. I didn't want to look like the one person who had something negative to say." I realized then I was making a mistake by perhaps not being as welcoming and open to controversial topics. If we are going to build a climate of mutual support, all stakeholders need to feel safe in expressing their concerns in an appropriate manner.

This is not to say we all get on a campaign to bash something or find something to gripe about in the name of improvement. On the contrary. I totally believe in the "glass-half-full" theory. If we open up the floodgates, we can always find something to complain about. Indeed, I need to wear my lens of solution-orientation and the lens of helpfulness as much as possible. We have only to look back at the example from Rath and Clifton (2004) about the Korean War to know that negativity is devastating. Add to that negativity the sometimes prevalent feeling among school personnel of helplessness and hopelessness, and you have a recipe for potential disaster. Teachers and school leaders can get caught up looking at all the things that are wrong in education (the kids aren't paying attention, the parents don't care, test scores are the focus, etc.) and begin to feel as though there is no choice to look at the bright side. So what happens? People who choose to focus on the negative walk around spreading poison among the others within their grasp. And poison does spread. I have experienced teachers in my office in tears because they just couldn't stand to work around negative people with their negative vibes any longer. I think about what I do to avoid poisonous snakes or poisonous scorpions (moving to Tucson, Arizona, recently has helped me learn a good bit about this topic). Do I go to the same lengths to avoid poisonous people or poisonous situations?

On the flipside are those who spread joy. One of my favorite activities to do on the first day of school every year was to have a short staff meeting to debrief the day. While there might be a couple of logistical items ("Can we remove that trash can blocking the door by the back hallway?" or "The air doesn't seem to be working on the west side of the school."), the bulk of the meeting was spent enjoying cookies and lemonade or cookies and milk (whichever after-school treat the staff seems to enjoy the most) and sharing stories of the day. I could always count on Vicki and Mary to be willing to share a hilarious story from the day. These stories would bring laughter and joy to everyone present, even to the hardest to please.

While positive thinking, filling each other's buckets, and laughter will take us through the rough times during a school year, people are going to experience real frustration sometimes. Take for example a school district that has initiated a new professional development protocol. Every teacher is required to write an individual improvement plan. The guidelines from the district are shared, plans are written in tandem with principal and coaching support, and the plans are uploaded to the electronic database. Two weeks later, the district sends an email to all staff saying, "Our electronic platform has been altered. Please make sure you redo your plan and upload the new one to the system in the next two weeks." Such a cacophony of frustration you have never heard. "We already did this, and now we have to do it again!" "They can't make us do it over again." "I spent hours on that."

I admit my reaction is to want to stifle the griping. Many educational leaders have a fear of griping. Griping leads to more griping and that can only mean bad news. But one humble lesson I have learned over my years in administration is that people need to gripe. So, I now advocate for a period of time in which I do not intervene in the griping, recognizing that everyone needs to vent. After a fair period of time, however, I might enlist the help of grade-level chairpersons to say, "Okay, let's all meet in my room and get your best complaint all ready." Once everyone has had a chance to let it go, we can then say, "The bottom line is we still have to do the thing we don't want to do." Whatever that thing is, we still have to do it, and the fact of the matter is, it isn't going to get done any quicker by more complaining.

And although I have worked with principals who believe in griping right back to their staff in an effort to show them they have problems, too, I disagree. If all the staff is upset, for example, that they have to redo their professional development plans, and I stand in front of them and say, "You all think you have it bad, you should see what I have to do!" I don't believe that is either professional or productive. As the leader of the school, the principal needs to put on the walk-in-the-muck boots and be ready for action without complaining to the troops. Tom Hanks in *Saving Private Ryan* (Spielberg, 1998) said it best, "I don't gripe to you, Reiben. I'm a Captain. We have a chain of command. Gripes go up, not down. Always up. You gripe to me, I gripe to my superior officer, and so on and so on and so on. I don't gripe to you. I don't gripe in front of you."

5. REMEMBER WHO WINS IF SUPPORT IS THERE
REMEMBER WHO LOSES IF SUPPORT IS NOT THERE

In summary of this section, school personnel must keep in mind our primary purpose: student progress and achievement. Bryk and Schneider (2002) interviewed staff from a school in Chicago, and everyone agreed they were there for the students. In fact, the principal even said he tried to represent the students in every decision he made. How staff members view others' decisions may be quite subjective, but if we keep the children front and center when we do whatever we do, I believe we can't stray too far off course.

E-Cubed: Effective Evaluation Example

How do you ensure the decisions staff members make are based primarily on the needs of students?

One suggestion is to use peer checks—when in doubt about what to do, check with two or three colleagues (not just your best friends but those whom you respect).

If we honestly believe in communicating with one another to build trust, then we will find a way to make time for it. We simply have to make communication one of our top priorities and then work toward that end. We need to put first things first. In this instance, a good example of putting first things first is making time for communication, even if it is difficult and time-consuming.

I encourage participants in my workshops to think about how they want the end of each conversation or encounter to be perceived when considering their own integrity and reputation. This habit implies we need to keep our eye on the end result we want, all the while making baby steps and strides toward that goal with consistency of practice. If, at the end of this conversation with a teacher, a teammate, or my supervisor, I want to end up with a relationship that is still intact and their view of me to be one of calm and reason and caring, then every moment I am in that conversation I should act with that calm, reason, and caring. I can't just say I want it but not act consistently with those behaviors.

We can broaden that view to say, "What do I want my students to say about me at the end of the school year?" Whatever that is we want them to say (she was fair, she cared about us, she taught our selves not just our minds, etc.), we need to do that thing every single day. We can't simply wait until May to turn on the charm.

We can broaden the view even further to say, "What do I want said about me at the end of my career?" Whether your role is one of a teacher, principal, or other staff member, what do you want people to say about you? A teacher I know retired a few years ago and during the send-off party, people stood up and said, "You were a good teacher" or "You were strong on discipline." When it was her turn to speak, she said, "I wonder why you have saved your compliments for my last day of teaching. There are some of you who haven't spoken to me in months, only to come in and wish me luck in my retirement." Two things are possibly at work here. First of all, if we want to know people appreciate our idea sharing at the end of our career, perhaps we should share ideas throughout our career. If we want to hear how we turned a tough student around, we should probably strive to do that every day, not just a one-time-shot of that. But, also, this retiring teacher had a point in a weird way. If we have a compliment for someone, or we believe someone has acted with character and integrity, we should tell them when we see it. Much like the premise of "Catch 'em being good," let's notice the good and recognize the good whenever we can.

Finally, we should ask, "What do I want said about me at my funeral or memorial service?" Whatever that is, we need to act with integrity in that manner now. It might be too late to "begin being good" tomorrow.

E-Cubed: Effective Evaluation Example

For what do you want to be remembered?

What is the legacy you will leave behind?

Whatever that thing is, use it as a lens through which to see each encounter with each person whose life you touch.

Make a list of your top five priorities in your school life.

How do you make sure you make time for those?

SUMMARY

Building trust during tough times is . . . well, tough. Is it possible to have a trust-filled organization when:

- Budgets are shrinking?
- Teacher observations and evaluations impact their pay?
- The public and the media seem to pile on the negative aspects of teaching?

This is not a trick question. The answer is, of course, YES, we have to believe that trust is possible even in the face of adversity. As a trainer in teacher evaluation, the question always arises: How am I supposed to live with an evaluation done by someone I don't trust? Likewise, principals will sometimes say, "I don't feel comfortable giving honest feedback because I don't trust that this teacher will be able to handle it." There seems to be a bit of an impasse in these examples. The fact of the matter is teacher observations and evaluations are meant to encourage improvement in the teaching process. If we are going to help people improve, there simply must be some expected modicum of trust present in order to accomplish the goal. Take, for example the teacher who says, "My principal has always given me feedback like 'Good job!' or 'Keep up the good work.' I know I need to give my students more specific feedback in order for them to grow. I need the same in my teaching practice."

Let's not just give this evaluation lip service. Let's truly make strides to improve teacher performance, which will ultimately improve student achievement.

Does trust build over time? One of the questions I wanted to research was, Is there a relationship between the number of years a teacher and principal have worked together and the perceived level of trust a teacher feels for the principal? Once again, the Omnibus Trust Scale was used, along with general demographic data provided by the teachers (including how many years they had taught and how many years they had worked for their current principal). In workshops, I always have participants guess the answer. Some say no, it doesn't matter. Others answer "yes, I guess trust grows over time." But inevitably, there is always that one person who looks skeptical the whole time and shakes his or her head in thought. When I call on them, they say something like, "I wonder if trust gets worse over time . . ."

Among the 518 people who answered both the length of time question and the trust survey itself, the highest overall level of trust in the principal was felt by the teachers who had worked for their current principal for less than one year, yielding an average rating of 4.71. The average rating on the same question by those teachers who had worked for their principal for more than 10 years was a 3.18. In fact, in other categories of time working for the current principal, the average ratings came nowhere near that of the less than 1-year category. Might trust be easy to initially gain but harder to maintain and keep over time? When I talked to my professors about my data, one of them said, "Over time, school leaders give teachers more time to watch us screw up." How depressing, I thought. Instead of focusing for too long on this seemingly negative statistic, I propose we move to solutions. Robert Eckert, the CEO of Mattel, once said, *"As you go to work, your top responsibility should be to build trust."* No matter what role we play in the school setting, as the school principal or a first-year teacher, I believe this edict is truer now than ever before. Within the school setting, we know that increased trust leads to better performance. It's simply easier to get things done with people with whom we have a higher level of trust.

In the classroom setting, teachers see this all the time. If students in the class are watchful and wary, they won't share during discussions, they won't feel free to ask questions, and they won't be able to complement each other on their good answers. Contrast that with a classroom filled with students and a teacher who feel free to complement one another, truly seem to enjoy one another's company, share openly in discussions, and ask questions when they don't understand the material. Danielson (2007) felt this aspect of classroom instruction was so critical, she devoted one entire domain of her framework for teaching to it. The classroom environment is dedicated to that feeling of respect and rapport and a pervasive view of the culture for learning. Underlying this entire domain is the aspect of trust: Can students trust the teacher to be fair and consistent? Can students trust the teacher to respond respectfully to questions, even if they seem like redundant or ignorant questions? If trust is built in classrooms, the actual act of instruction will be made wholly easier from the start and exponentially increase over time. If all our classrooms were built on trust between teacher and students and among students themselves, how could test scores and, more importantly, deep understanding of concepts, not take place?

So, how can schools stay motivated to support each other and continue to focus on relationships and trust? Barbara Glanz, a national motivational speaker, tells this story about Johnny the Bagger, a story that has now been included in the motivational speeches of businesses all over the world.

> *A few years ago, I was hired by a large Supermarket chain to lead a customer service program—to build customer loyalty. During my speech I said, "Every one of you can make a difference and create memories for your customers that will motivate them to come back." How?*
>
> *Put your personal signature on the job. Think about something you can do for your customer to make them feel special—a memory that will make them come back.*
>
> *About a month after I had spoken, I received a phone call from a 19-year-old bagger named Johnny. He proudly informed me he was a Down syndrome individual and told me his story.*
>
> *"I liked what you talked about," he said, "but at first I didn't think I could do anything special for our customers."*
>
> *"After all I'm just a bagger. Then I had an Idea," Johnny said.*
>
> *"Every night after work, I'd come home and find a thought for the day."*
>
> *"If I can't find a saying I like," he added, "I'd just think one up."*
>
> *When Johnny had a good thought for the day, his dad helped him set it up on the computer and print multiple copies. Johnny cut out each quote and signed the back. Then he'd bring them to work the next day.*
>
> *"When I finish bagging someone's groceries, I put my thought for the day in their bag and say, thanks for shopping with us."*

> *It touched me to think that this young man—with a job most people would say is not important—had made it important by creating precious memories for all of his customers. A month later the store manager called me . . .*
>
> *"You won't believe what happened. When I was making my rounds today, I found Johnny's checkout line was three times longer than anyone else's."*
>
> *"It went all the way down the frozen food aisle. So I quickly announced, 'we need more cashiers; get more lanes open,' as I tried to get people to change lanes.*
>
> *But no one would move."*
>
> *They said, "No that's OK—we want to be in Johnny's lane. We want his thought for the day."*
>
> *The store manager continued, "It was a joy to watch Johnny delight the customers."*
>
> *"I got a lump in my throat when one woman said, 'I used to shop at your store once a week, but now I come by every time I go by, because I want to get Johnny's thought for the day.'"*
>
> *A few months later, the manager called me again.*
>
> *"Johnny has transformed our store. Now when the floral department has a broken flower or unused corsage, they find and elderly women or a little girl and pin it on them. Everyone has had a lot of fun creating memories. Our customers are talking about us . . . they're coming back and bringing their friends."*

We need to make our schools places where everyone, including the staff themselves, wants to come into our school like everyone wanted to come into Johnny's lane. In order to make that happen, we need to care about the good, look for the good, and celebrate when we see the good. This may sound like a simple affair, but for anyone who has tried to focus on the good for a week-long challenge, much less a year or a career-long challenge, you know I am not suggesting something simple or minimal. Looking for the good in our work takes work, but it is work that is truly worth it.

What are some ways we can start today to build up a school that is known for its communication, honesty, support, character, competence, and overall trust?

1. *Be willing to trust and be trusted.* Just this week, I read an article on msn.com about the most trusted and least trusted Hollywood celebrities. I did not find it surprising to see that Kristen Stewart from *Twilight* fame was ranked least likely to be trusted from female

actors. Why do you think that might be? I think it's because we general public folks find very little "open" about Stewart. If an emotional bank account is required to establish a relationship with people, there is not much emotional bank account built up with someone who shows so little emotion and feeling, even if it is from behind a camera. Take a guess as to the least trusted male actor. Tom Cruise. I attribute this to another phenomenon, one of too many past mistakes. Just to finish out this analogy, try the question below.

THINKING ABOUT TRUST

In a May 2013 msn.com Internet poll, which actor and actress were revealed to be the "most trusted" celebrities?

(Tom Hanks and Sandra Bullock)

Why do you think that is?

---

2. *Let go of resentments. Forgive.* We all make mistakes. It is likely that every one of us has done something in our lives that we regret. Perhaps it is talking about someone behind their back. Maybe you made a promise that you were unable to keep. Perhaps it is getting into a disagreement with someone and not feeling comfortable resolving it. While those errors in judgment sometimes have significant consequences, I think it's safe to say no one wants to be defined by his or her mistakes. If we don't want others defining us based on an error in their judgment of us, then we might want to think about not doing this to others.

One good strategy in allowing ourselves to trust while reserving judgment until later is, trust but verify. Ronald Reagan has been credited with saying this, but it is now a mantra heard all over corporations across the country. In other words, a teacher can trust that her teammate is going to make copies of the newsletter that needs to go home to all parents tonight, but if she hasn't received the copies by an hour before dismissal, she might want to check on her teammate.

Likewise, the team counting on a staff member to call and reserve the picnic tables for a field trip can simply ask, a week out, "Hey, just checking on the picnic tables. Did reserving that go okay?"

The point is, we need to trust folks to make good and right decisions and actions and be willing to forgive them if they flub up every once in a while. Alvin Toffler said, "The illiterate of the 21st century will not be those who cannot read and write but those who cannot learn, unlearn, and relearn." Mistrust sometimes stems from growing up in a low-trust environment. Perhaps some people have experienced more than their fair share of untrustworthy people at work and in personal relationships. But a Latin proverb says, "It is equally an error to trust all men or no man." Trust comes with an inherent risk, especially if an already trusting relationship has not been firmly established. But we can't allow mistrust and resentments to cloud our everyday work, especially in schools.

I've heard it said that harboring resentments against others is like taking poison and waiting for the other person to die. First of all, it simply doesn't make good sense to hold onto resentments. Some people for whom we harbor ill feelings have no idea we are upset or why we feel the way we feel. Others, even if they do have a clue, might not care as much as we do, and therefore, we are allowing their behaviors to live rent free in our heads and hearts. Not to mention that holding in angry feelings toward a teammate, supervisor, or supervisee can lead to possible health problems.

Can we afford to let go of a resentment, fearing the person who wronged us will think they have "gotten away with something"? I would venture to say we can't afford not to.

3. *Begin with the end in mind. If you ultimately want a trusting relationship, you must do it every day.* I just read a quote by Michael Josephson (2012) that says, "People of character do the right thing even if no one else does, not because they think it will change the world but because they refuse to be changed by the world."

My best example of this scenario in place is in working as a teacher, counselor, or principal with families who have recently divorced. We know it when we see the absence of trust—the backstabbing, agenda-seeking behavior that only ends up harming the child for whom we are meeting in the first place. But consider the flipside of that behavior. Parents who, despite not being able to see fit to stay married to one another, realize their child(ren) are the ones who will win or lose depending on the behavior of the parents. When we remain on the same page for the good of the children despite differences, everyone wins.

These are tall orders, not at all easy. But we simply must commit to the work if we want to reap the benefits of working in a school filled with trust. In the words of F. Scott Fitzgerald, "Being grown up is a terribly hard thing to do. It is much easier to go from one childhood to another."

Bryk and Schneider (2002) conclude that trust is actually a resource needed for school improvement. As important as technology, curriculum materials, and a cafeteria, trust is essential to growth and maintaining a level of comfort in which all participants are eager to share and grow. If we take the time to nurture trust and nurture people, the climate will most certainly improve.

In the Rod Stewart song, "Forever Young," he sings about being courageous and brave as advice for becoming a strong adult. I can think of no other work that is more courageous or brave than to begin to build, regain, or sustain trust in a school. It may be hard work, but it is so worth it. We need to balance the heart with the head. Let's make sure we do the right thing for the right reasons as consistently as possible.

References

Arneson, M. S. (2012). *Character and competence: A mixed methods study on teacher trust in principals in a mid-sized county in Florida* (Doctoral dissertation). University of West Florida.

Arneson, S. (2011a). *Communicate and motivate: The school leader's guide to effective communication.* New York, NY: Eye on Education.

Arneson, S. (2011b). *Letting go of K.C.* Barbourville, Kentucky: Martin Sisters.

Bies, R., & Tripp, T. (1996). Beyond distrust: "Getting even" and the need for revenge. In R. M. Kramer & T. R. Tyler (Eds.), *Trust in organizations: Frontiers and theory of research* (pp. 302–330). Thousand Oaks, CA: Sage.

Brimhall, J. (2010). *The effects of individual communicator styles on perceived faculty trust* (Doctoral dissertation). Retrieved from ProQuest Dissertations and Theses database. (UMI No. 3398653)

Bryk, A. S., & Schneider, B. (2002). *Trust in schools: A core resource for school reform.* New York, NY: Russell Sage Foundation.

Bryk, A. S., & Schneider, B. (2003). Trust in schools: A core resource for school reform. *Educational Leadership, 60*(6), 40–44.

Clark, M. C., & Payne, R. L. (2006). Character-based determinants of trust in leaders. *Risk Analysis, 26*(5), 1161–1173. doi:10.1111/j.1539–6924.2006.00823.x

Covey, S. M. R., & Merrill, R. R. (2006). *The speed of trust: The one thing that changes everything.* New York, NY: Free Press.

Covey, S. M. R., & Merrill, R. R. (2012). *Smart trust: Creating prosperity, energy and joy in a low-trust world.* New York, NY: Free Press.

Covey, S. R. (1989). *The seven habits of highly effective people: Powerful lessons in personal change.* New York, NY: Free Press.

Danielson, C. (2007). *Enhancing professional practice: A framework for teaching.* Alexandria, VA: ASCD.

Farmer, A. (2010). *The perception of teachers and principals on leaders' behavior informed by 13 core competencies and its relationship to teacher motivation* (Doctoral dissertation). Retrieved from ProQuest Dissertations and Theses database. (UMI No. 3448248)

Feltman, C. (2009). *The thin book of trust.* Bend, OR: The Thin Book.

Hall, L. A. (2006). *A framework for building and promoting trust: A case study of an Illinois middle level school focusing on the leadership behaviors of the principal* (Doctoral dissertation). Retrieved from ProQuest Dissertations and Theses database. (UMI No. 3223605)

Himmele, P., & Himmele, W. (2011). *Total participation techniques: Making every student an active learner.* Alexandria, VA: ASCD.

Hoy, W. K., & Tschannen-Moran, M. (2003). The conceptualization and measurement of faculty trust in schools: The omnibus T-scale. In W. K. Hoy & C. G. Miskel (Eds.), *Studies in leading and organizing schools* (pp. 181–208). Greenwich, CT: Information Age.

Jones, R. (2007). *The principal's role in building teacher leadership capacity in high-performing elementary schools: A qualitative case study* (Doctoral dissertation). Retrieved from ProQuest Dissertations and Theses database. (UMI No. 3292559)

Josephson, M. (2012). Retrieved from https://whatwillmatter.com/2012/10/quote-people-of-character-do-the-right-thing-even-if-no-one-else-does-not-because-they-think-it-will-change-the-world-but-because-they-refuse-to-be-changed-by-the-world-michael-josephson/

Kagy, L. (2010). *Teacher trust and leadership behaviors used by elementary school principals* (Doctoral dissertation). Retrieved from ProQuest Dissertations and Theses database. (UMI No. 3411165)

Lipton, L., & Wellman, B. (2013). *Learning-focused supervision.* Arlington, MA: MiraVia.

Marzano, R. (2003). *What works in schools: Translating research into action.* Alexandria, VA: ASCD.

Mayer, R. C., Davis, J. H, & Schoorman, F. D. (1995). An integration model of organizational trust. *Academy of Management: The Academy of Management Review, 20*(3), 709–734. Retrieved from ABI/INFORM Global. (Document ID: 6693112)

McGregor, D. (1960). *The human side of enterprise.* New York, NY: McGraw-Hill.

National Conference on State Legislatures. (2006). No Child Left Behind Act of 2001. Retrieved from http://www.ncsl.org/programs/educ/NCLB history.htm

Noddings, N. (2005). Care and moral education. In H. S. Shapiro & D. E. Purpel (Eds.), *Critical social issues in American education* (pp. 297–308). Nahwah, NJ: Lawrence Erlbaum.

Rath, T., & Clifton, D. (2004). *How full is your bucket?* New York, NY: Gallup Press.

Reina, D. S., & Reina, M. L. (n.d.). Retrieved from https://www.asaecenter.org/Resources/ANowDetail.cfm?ItemNumber=16982

Reina, D. S., & Reina, M. L. (2006). *Trust and betrayal in the workplace: Building effective relationships in your organization.* San Francisco, CA: Berret-Koehler.

Roberts, J. (2011, March 24). Governor's tenure reform bill for teachers passes House. *The Commercial Appeal.* Retrieved from http://www.commercialappeal.com/news/2011/mar/24/governors-tenure-reform-bill-teachers-passes-house/

Rothenberger, S. (2008). Developing a leadership company: From leadership behavior to leadership responsibilities. *Problems and Perspectives in Management, 6*(1), 56–63.

Rowland, K. (2008). *The relationship of principal leadership and teacher morale* (Doctoral dissertation). Retrieved from ProQuest Dissertations and Theses database. (UMI No. 3297821)

Schnall, R. (2009). *When teachers talk: Principal abuse of teachers.* Chicago, IL: Goldenring Publishing, LLC.

Sergiovanni, T. J. (1995). *The principalship: A reflective practice perspective.* Needham Heights, MA: Allyn and Bacon.

Spielberg, S. [Director]. (1998). *Saving Private Ryan* [Film]. United States: DreamWorks Pictures.

Stimson, H. L. (n.d.). Retrieved from http://www.quotationspage.com/quote/3003.html

Survey Monkey. (n.d.). Retrieved from http://www.surveymonkey.com/s/BXWLG56

Tschannen-Moran, M. (1998). *Trust and collaboration in urban elementary schools* (Doctoral dissertation). Retrieved from ProQuest Dissertations and Theses database. (UMI No. 9900923)

Turner, E. (2010). *A correlational study of trust in an organization undergoing change* (Doctoral dissertation). Retrieved from ProQuest Dissertations and Theses database. (UMI No. 3414564)

Vodicka, D. (2006). The four elements of trust. *Principal Leadership (Middle School Ed.), 7*(3), 27–30.

Whitaker, T. (2008). *What great principals do differently: 15 things that matter the most.* New York, NY: Routledge.

Whitaker, T. (2011). *Shifting the monkey: The art of protecting good people from liars, criers, and other slackers.* Bloomington, IN: Triple Nickel Press.

Wong, H. (2004). *The first days of school: How to be an effective teacher.* Mountain View, CA: Harry Wong Publications.

Zimmerman, S. (2003). Five steps for improving teacher evaluation: Focusing on the continual improvement of teaching and learning. *The Professional Educator, 25*(2), 43–53. Retrieved from http://www.theprofessionaleducator.org/

Index

A SAGE Company

Corwin is committed to improving education for all learners by publishing books and other professional development resources for those serving the field of PreK–12 education. By providing practical, hands-on materials, Corwin continues to carry out the promise of its motto: **"Helping Educators Do Their Work Better."**